Routledge Revivals

Foundations of Faith Volume 3

Originally published in 1926, this is the third of four volumes to discuss Christian Theology, under the guidance of the historic decisions of the Christian Church and the prevailing tendencies of Catholic thought in the early 20th Century. This volume is concerned with the Church, considering questions of authority and what is meant by 'Catholic'.

Foundations of Faith Volume 3
Ecclesiological

W.E. Orchard

First published in 1926 by George Allen & Unwin Ltd.

This edition first published in 2024 by Routledge
4 Park Square, Milton Park, Abingdon, Oxon, OX14 4RN

and by Routledge
605 Third Avenue, New York, NY 10158.

Routledge is an imprint of the Taylor & Francis Group, an informa business

© 1926 W.E. Orchard.

The right of W.E. Orchard to be identified as the author of this work has been asserted by him in accordance with sections 77 and 78 of the Copyright, Designs and Patents Act 1988.

All rights reserved. No part of this book may be reprinted or reproduced or utilised in any form or by any electronic, mechanical, or other means, now known or hereafter invented, including photocopying and recording, or in any information storage or retrieval system, without permission in writing from the publishers.

ISBN 13: 978-1-032-89991-6 (hbk)
ISBN 13: 978-1-003-54567-5 (ebk)
ISBN 13: 978-1-032-89997-8 (pbk)
Book DOI 10.4324/9781003545675

FOUNDATIONS OF FAITH

III
ECCLESIOLOGICAL

BY THE
REV. W. E. ORCHARD, D.D.

LONDON: GEORGE ALLEN & UNWIN LTD.
RUSKIN HOUSE, 40 MUSEUM STREET, W.C. 1

Printed in Great Britain by
UNWIN BROTHERS, LIMITED, LONDON AND WOKING

First published in 1926

(All rights reserved)

FOREWORD

THE previous publication of each chapter of this book as a monthly tract may partially explain the necessity, even if it cannot dispense with an apology, for having to ask the reader to note the list of corrections given below; for a second revision was generally impossible before the final printing had to be undertaken. The controversy already awakened by the publication of some of the Tracts, notably those on The Catholic Church and The Eucharist, does not augur too well for the reception of the book as a whole. But perhaps the author may be permitted to claim that he has given considerable thought to the subject, and that he has endeavoured to formulate a theory which shall be true to spiritual principles, takes note of historical developments, and holds out some hope of reconciling divergent positions; he may therefore be allowed to beg that reviewers will really read the book, critics will seriously consider the whole situation, and those who reject the position here reached will

FOUNDATIONS OF FAITH

not be content with simple rejection, but endeavour themselves to formulate a better solution which the past gives some hope that the future may realise.

W. E. O.

CORRECTIONS

Page 73, line 14, read : *opposite from that which was,* instead of, *opposite that was.*

Page 111, line 2, read : *natural* instead of, *national.*

Page 115, line 24, read : *It may be withdrawn* instead of, *they may be withdrawn.*

Page 129, line 24, read : *corruption* instead of, *conception.*

Page 164, line 7, read : *mediately* instead of, *immediately.*

CONTENTS

	PAGE
FOREWORD	v
THE HOLY SPIRIT AND THE CHURCH	1
THE APOSTOLIC CHURCH	17
THE CATHOLIC CHURCH	33
THE HOLINESS OF THE CHURCH	49
THE UNITY OF THE CHURCH	65
AUTHORITY	81
THE SACRAMENTAL SYSTEM	97
THE EUCHARIST	113
RITUAL	129
THE CHURCH AND THE SOCIAL ORDER	145
THE CATHOLIC CHURCH AND INTERNATIONALISM	161
THE CHURCH AND HUMANITY	177

I
THE HOLY SPIRIT AND THE CHURCH

THE vagueness and confusion of modern religious thought is particularly noticeable in its conception of the Holy Spirit. The theological speculation of our time, throwing off the guidance of the traditional interpretation of the Church, prefers to explain the Holy Spirit as nothing more than a special name for the influence of God, as that is felt by the heart, or is manifested in the rise of spiritual life. And with this religious outlook the Church seems an unnecessary institution, which attempts to capture and confine the Spirit, and would quench it altogether, were it not that the Spirit, driven out, finds a welcome and a response in individuals and movements outside the Church. The reaction from these conditions, in the absence of the peculiar experience of the Spirit promised through the worship and fellowship of the Church, only confirms vague conceptions of the Spirit; so that low ideas of the Church and impersonal conceptions of the Holy Spirit go together and have a reciprocal effect.

Such explanations naturally tend to shade down into, and come to be identified with, the conception of spirit as it is so commonly used in modern idealistic terminology, where it stands rather for the ethical essence or flavour of a thing. This usage deserves a more careful description, for it is at the root of a great deal of modern confusion. For instance, the "spirit" is often placed in contradistinction to the "letter"; and since by the letter

THE HOLY SPIRIT AND THE CHURCH

is meant the definite form of an idea, the spirit means the idea itself, which might be expressed in a different form; or some still vaguer feeling, which does not even need to be expressed at all. Under this influence, the spirit of Jesus comes to mean, neither the Holy Spirit in the New Testament sense, nor the active spiritual presence of Jesus, but rather the ethical essence of His teaching, His general attitude and outlook towards life, the feel of His disposition and character. This inevitably becomes something entirely human and subjective, for it is now nothing more than a distillation of His mind, character and teaching; our understanding of Him, rather than a living, personal influence acting upon ourselves. Thus the frequent appeal to the spirit of Jesus, in protest against dogmas and formulas, is often only an appeal to a subjective standard; and although it seems to promise a much wider basis for agreement, it does so only because it really allows everyone to make his own interpretation; which leaves people much as they were before. No doubt a very wide and comprehensive Church could be founded upon a confession of loyalty, and a promise to live according to the spirit of Jesus; but there would be almost no theological, moral or practical issue which would not rend such a Church into as many fragments as there were persons. Wherever this conception of the Spirit came to be accepted, it would be only natural to find that the idea of the Church had been correspondingly lowered. Under the influence of such ideas the Church is bound to become a purely voluntary association; that is, something which a Christian might, but need not join. Such an institution must be regarded as a purely human necessity, and not indeed a necessity for everyone, and least of all for persons with a strong sense of immediate spiritual guidance. A further stage in the lowering of the idea is then inevitable, and has already been reached, namely, that any kind of organization must be detrimental to, and perhaps even destructive of, the spirit, which must be left free if wider and further manifestation is to be gained. So we reach the popular, but pessimistic statement, which has become erected into a kind of anti-ecclesiastical dogma : " the idea creates the organization, and then the organization destroys the idea."

There can be little need to enforce the point that whether these conceptions are alone acceptable to the modern mind, and these tendencies inevitable to modern religious feeling and anti-dogmatic speculation, this is not the New Testament conception of the Holy Spirit, and this is not the New Testament idea of the Church. To take the former point first : in the New Testament the Holy Spirit is indisputably personal. There is hardly a reference that could bear any other than a personal meaning, or could be taken to describe an influence merely felt, and not vitally impressed ; still less is there much indication of the use of the word " spirit " in the modern sense as an ethical essence, a general attitude, or a formless idea. The Holy Spirit can not only be quenched, but grieved ; He not only bears witness, but intercedes ; things seem good to Him, as to us. In the second place, the personality of the Spirit is distinguished alike from the Father and from the Son as another. Not only are the three Persons distinctly mentioned in connection with the Baptism of Jesus; the Holy Ghost descends upon Jesus, and He is characterized as anointed with the Holy Ghost, which cannot mean that He was anointed with Himself ; while Jesus regards the Spirit as " another " Paraclete whom He Himself will send in His place. It would be ad-

THE HOLY SPIRIT AND THE CHURCH

mitted that, in the Epistles, these three, the Father, the Son and the Holy Ghost, are constantly mentioned alongside one another as distinct, as on an equality, and yet as in some vital connection. This latter point is emphasized not only by the way in which the action of the one is made necessary to the revelation of, or access to the other, but in the fact that the Holy Spirit is sometimes called the Spirit of God and sometimes the Spirit of Jesus. But a similar connection is found in the Fourth Gospel, for while Jesus there promises that He will send the Spirit to His followers as a consolation for His own departure, He also promises that He Himself will return to dwell with them, and then not alone, but with the Father. It would be wrong to infer that there is ever a confusion of the Persons, and perhaps too much to claim that their functions are interchangeable ; but so close is the connection that we are compelled to believe that Father, Son and Spirit are so united that no one of them ever acts apart from the other ; and they are so like in person as to be interpretative of one another. In this material, the doctrine of a Trinity of persons with unity of substance, and even the doctrine of the *Filioque*, namely, that the Spirit proceeds from the Father *and* the Son, seem to be involved and are absolutely necessary to any orderly or satisfying thought which claims to be based on the New Testament.

But equally necessary and concrete is the New Testament idea of the Church. Whether the Church was founded by Jesus is not to be made dependent upon the two solitary references in which the word " Church " is found in St. Matthew's Gospel, or upon any decision concerning the authenticity of the famous text, " Thou art Peter, and upon this rock will I build my Church." The excision of this text, on

THE HOLY SPIRIT AND THE CHURCH

the ground that it is found in St. Matthew alone, can plead no valid canon of criticism; the assumption that it is a later addition is supported by no manuscript, and the feeling of its being due to later ecclesiastical development is simply due to the use of the word " church." If the words are translated back to the Aramaic original, all feeling of lateness vanishes; for " church " (Gr. *ecclesia*) is a word already used for the " assembly " or congregation in the Old Testament, as well as for Israel as a whole. The other passage in St. Matthew, where the disciples are told to report the case of the obstinate brother to the church, may possibly not refer to the Christian Church, but to the Jewish Assembly then in being and in possession of judicial functions. In the Petrine reference, moreover, it should be noted that Jesus refers to " my church," which evidently distinguishes it from the Jewish Church, while He speaks of its building as if it were still in the future. But the attitude of Jesus, in choosing the twelve apostles, and in committing to them special responsibilities and powers, is a sanction of organization, and at least a preparation for the creation of the Church. And from the Acts of the Apostles we should infer that the Church was not regarded as in existence until the outpouring of the Holy Spirit at Pentecost. If we examine the use of the word " church " in the rest of the New Testament, we must come to the conclusion that it was a definite body, so definite as able to be called the Body of Christ; its " members " are referred to, so that it is obviously perfectly clear, first, where the Church exists, and secondly, who belongs to it. In the New Testament the Church is a definite organization, and any idea that a person could be a Christian without belonging to the Church, or without the recognition of the Church, falls utterly outside its conception. It is true that the word " church " is used in three distinct senses : it is used, first of all, of the actual assembly or meeting together of Christians ; it is used also of the whole Body of Christ, that is all those who belong to, because they are accustomed to meet in the assembly ; and it is used of any particular local assembly, and in the same double sense, namely, the assembly itself when actually meeting, and those who are members of it. It is a confirmatory indication of the concreteness of the Church that when its emergence is described in the Acts of the Apostles we hear about its numbers : first of all we have the number of disciples given before Pentecost, about one hundred and twenty ; then we hear of the eleven apostles, and of Matthias being numbered with them ; and then we are told that, as a result of Pentecost, there were added to them about three thousand souls.

Nevertheless, both in regard to the Holy Spirit, and in regard to the Church, these clear-cut distinctions of the New Testament fail to cover the whole ground, or to provide a sufficient definition, once analytic thought is applied to the subject, or questions that history has made necessary are raised. Let us therefore return again, first of all, to the conception of the Holy Spirit. It must be admitted that the Person and work of the Holy Spirit remain somewhat vague, despite all that theological exposition has been able to do. In the doctrine of the Trinity the necessity for three Persons, and especially for the third Person, has always remained somewhat difficult to account for. In Augustine's famous argument for the Trinity, as being traceable to the necessity of Love, and his identification of the Holy Spirit with the love which exists between the Father and the Son, it is obvious that in this we have only a functional principle, and nothing necessarily

THE HOLY SPIRIT AND THE CHURCH

personal. We probably approximate somewhat nearer to this necessity, when it is recognized that a third person is necessary if love is to be more than mutual, and shall embrace agreement in love; and the number three does seem to provide a combination of perfection with irreducible simplicity. But further than that we cannot go, and we simply have to rest upon the revelation that there are three, and only three, as well as recognize that it is not in man's mind to prescribe the necessities of the divine Love, while we can infer from the constant threefoldness of all things, that this is due to all things being made by and according to the divine Mind.

But while the necessity of the third Person must perhaps remain imperfectly apprehended by us, the vagueness that surrounds our conception of Him can be traced in part to the gradual development between the Old and New Testament representations of the Holy Spirit. It must be admitted that, in the Old Testament, the Spirit of God is not conceived as personally distinct from God, and could not, of course, be so represented without a further revelation of the distinction of Persons in the Godhead. It is only under the teaching, and after the ministry of Jesus that the Spirit is recognized as a distinct Person. But it is interesting to notice how even in the New Testament the Spirit of God seems to work upon two levels. In order to come to God at all, it is regarded as absolutely necessary to possess the Spirit; it is declared that no one can confess Jesus Christ apart from the Spirit's aid; and yet the baptism of the Holy Ghost is the gift of God, and can only come upon those who believe in Christ. It is obvious from this that the Spirit of God must be present in some degree to the human heart, for wherever man seeks after God it is by His inspiration and aid. The confession of Jesus Christ marks

THE HOLY SPIRIT AND THE CHURCH

a further stage in responding to the Spirit's inspiration, the Spirit alone being able truly and fully to recognize the divine Person of Christ. But when that has been confessed, there follows a far deeper sense of God within, which is recognized as an indwelling of the Godhead, now known and distinguished as Father, Son and Holy Spirit. A further stage is probably discernible in what is called the *baptism* of the Holy Ghost, which is the peculiar gift of the Church, and is the conveying of the original Pentecostal outpouring by those who themselves received it; for it is noticeable that while there may have been an acknowledgment of Jesus Christ, and an acceptance of Him, the baptism of the Holy Ghost does not occur apart from the action of members of the Church.

Now it is at this point, where the Holy Spirit and the Church are linked together, that we may find much needed illumination and understanding. It has been noted by someone that we have no imaginative conception of the Holy Spirit, of His form or character; whereas we have of that of Jesus. But neither have we any such conception of the Father, save in so far as we know that in the face of Jesus we see the glory of God, so that those who contemplate the character of Christ have seen the Father. It is precisely the same with the Holy Spirit; we have no knowledge of His personality or character, save that it is like that of Jesus. This is because it is the definite purpose of the Spirit to conceal Himself; first of all, in order that He may the more closely penetrate the human heart by His inspiration and so lead men to truth, only as the heart responds fully disclosing Himself; so that, to the incompletely awakened, the inspiration of the Spirit may be active and yet referred by the individual to his own thoughts and aspirations.

Secondly, it is the purpose of the Spirit to point always away from Himself, to take of the things of Jesus, and to bring us to the Father. But another cause of a certain element of vagueness clinging to the conception of the Spirit is bound up with the fact that the Spirit does not reveal Himself fully to the individual, but only in the Church. The Church is the sphere of His complete revelation, and only through the Church, therefore, can we gain a clear idea of the Spirit's personality and power. Therefore the Spirit can only be fully revealed as the Church becomes perfectly one, holy and universal. The presence of the Spirit may be particularly felt, however, when the Church is actually assembled; not only in the more mystical fellowship of worship, or in the impression that may accompany spiritual preaching, but when the Church is specially assembled to seek after the truth by conference and prayer. Therefore, as the story of the Church is not yet finished, so a fuller realization of the Holy Spirit has yet to be attained; and this is the cause of the lack of clear understanding and still remaining vagueness. It is in the realm of the Holy Spirit, both through the illumination of truth and the endowment of power, that progress is open and exploration needed.

But this vagueness on the one hand, with the promise of further disclosure on the other, are both necessary, if we are to understand the wider work of the Spirit and His central purpose of building up the Church. If we take the teaching of the Bible as a whole, we shall be able to discern how the Spirit is closely bound up with all manifestations of life. It was the Spirit of God moving upon the face of the waters that began the movement of light, order and life in the inanimate world and set it upon its wonderful and still unfinished develop-

THE HOLY SPIRIT AND THE CHURCH

ment. The Spirit of God is still more intimately concerned with the development of man's own spirit; his reason, his skill, and his artistic powers are specially ascribed to the Spirit, and, later, the manifestation of what is more definitely called inspiration. It is no disproof of the ultimate source of such manifestations that modern psychology should regard many of those early manifestations, such as we find in early prophetic utterances in the Old Testament, or even perhaps such a phenomenon as the speaking with tongues, or the display of other psychic powers in the New Testament, as due, on the one hand, to deep disturbances of man's mind, or, on the other, to the heightened influence of mass suggestion. These might well be the first effects of the Spirit's more intimate touch upon the mind of man. But we move to a higher plane in the recognition of the indwelling Spirit when we recognize the Spirit in Jesus, and the confession of His divinity opens a man's mind to the wide area of congruous religious truth, makes him more susceptible to inspired aspirations, and sheds abroad the love of God in his heart; the identification of the Holy Spirit by the image of Jesus, and the interpretation of Christ's Godhead, naturally influencing, deepening and confirming one another. Then in and through the fellowship of the Church the Spirit gains ever firmer ground, greater clearness, and higher power in the soul of man. Therefore it can be understood how it is the ultimate aim of the Spirit to draw men together into one body in order that they may become the Body of Christ, included in His glorified humanity, and thereby lifted by and with Him into the glory of the Godhead. For this destiny is not for individual souls as such, but only as they are united together in union with Christ.

THE HOLY SPIRIT AND THE CHURCH

Therefore the idea of some fundamental opposition between spirit and body, the Holy Spirit and the Church, is seen to be utterly false. So close is the connection between the Spirit and the body that the unity of the Church is dependent upon the unity of the Spirit; there is one body and one Spirit. It is only when the Spirit is imperfectly obeyed, and the need for using other minds to reinforce, and complement, and correct our own, is not understood, that there is thought to be any antagonism between the Spirit and the body. The body does not confine or contain the Spirit, but is the medium by which the Spirit can make Himself more clearly and strongly felt. It does not mean, therefore, that the inspiration of the Spirit is limited to the Church, or that men outside the Church receive nothing from Him. But it is towards the Church that the Spirit of God works, bringing souls to confess Jesus and uniting them to the Church. Once this recognition of the antecedent and extra-ecclesiastical work of the Holy Spirit is recognized, and yet its ultimate aim is also admitted, many of the difficulties which the modern religious mind has felt on this subject grow less weighty.

No doubt it is largely through the clash between spiritual movements and the inertia of the organized body, which have taken place in connection with the development of religion and the history of the Church, that the idea of an essential opposition between the Spirit and the body has emerged and has become so widespread in our own times. If we recognize, as we are bound to do, the operation of the Spirit outside the Church, the evidence of His work in solitary individuals and even in widespread spiritual movements would be expected and should be welcomed; though we might expect that the career of such individuals or such movements, if

THE HOLY SPIRIT AND THE CHURCH

brought into touch with the Church at all, would coalesce with it. Otherwise we should expect those individuals to appear somewhat sporadically and leave no succession, or the religious movements which failed to establish contact with the Church to perish, as it were, in the sands, or become a stagnant, diminishing unhealthy swamp. And if the historic Church itself provides any standard for comparison, that is precisely what we do find. What is more difficult to explain is the rise of movements within the Church which have been met with opposition on the part of the authorities, and have broken away in order to obtain freedom for the fuller following of the Spirit; for this seems to show evidence of a lack of spiritual discernment on the part of the organized body. One of these movements arose very early in the history of the Church, and is known as Montanism. It was a protest against a growing officialism and an endeavour to return to the prophetic freedom of the Church's early days. As a movement it can hardly fail to gain sympathy from any spiritually-minded observer, and all down history there have been movements of this kind. It is no evidence for spiritual discernment, but the very contrary, not to see in the early days, say, of the Reformation, the Wesleyan movement, or the Salvation Army, manifestations of real spiritual leading and power; but these movements must, nevertheless, also come under the judgment of history, and if we watch them certain tendencies become manifest. This is not the place to speak of the errors into which they may have fallen, for that raises the whole question of the standard of truth and authority which must be dealt with fully at a later stage. But the most sympathetic could not but admit a certain element of extravagance, a lack of restraint, an impatience with more sober ways

THE HOLY SPIRIT AND THE CHURCH

and the ordinary workings of the Spirit; and even if this demands reference to some standard and raises again the question of authority, there are objective manifestations which do not raise this issue, namely, the dying down of spiritual power within those very movements which seem to have been initially inspired by the Spirit. And, what is equally important, these movements, which broke away from the restraint of the old body in order to gain more perfect freedom for the spontaneous manifestation of the Spirit, eventually became organized, and have, in degree, only copied the organization they first protested against, or have created another even more highly developed and less specially fitted organization. Despite the harshness and blindness of authoritative action, which may be accounted equally guilty for the separation from the main body which occurred, and the serious loss which the Church itself must have suffered, there must be taken into account the extraordinary tenacity of the main body, its maintenance of the balance of truth, and its eventual recovery from the loss sustained. The Church can often be recognized to have learned something from the movements which separated from it, while, despite the darkness and deadness which may have followed, there break forth at length fresh signs of light and life. It is bound to be concluded that, on the whole, apart from spasmodic movements, and when other overflowings of the Spirit have died down, the Spirit does seem to reside in the fullest sense and most persistent power within the main body; and it is there that responsibility, continuity and, consequently, hope for the future remain. We may go further and notice also that even where there has been a breach with the main body, it is in those movements which organized themselves in

THE HOLY SPIRIT AND THE CHURCH

some degree on the old ecclesiastical model, that the spiritual movement has continued longest and maintains a more frequent manifestation of power. Nothing is more symptomatic of our times than the frequent rise, but as frequent disappearance, of religious movements intended to supplement or supersede the Church, whose career only confirms the general lesson gained from history. It does not need to be argued that the Church, in its present condition at any rate, is a perfect instrument for the Spirit, any more than we need to hold that it is the Spirit's only instrument. But it is here that the Spirit continues to act with a combination of greater purity, perseverance and permanence. Therefore the Spirit can be regarded as a body-building Spirit whose chief work is seen in His gathering men together in order to make them members of one body, progressively responsive to His guidance and illumination.

There is no evidence, therefore, that a more complete abandonment of the Church idea would lead to a fuller spiritual development, because of the absolute freedom which would then be gained; or that where the movements that have broken away from the Church have erred has been in their preserving in any degree the methods and model from which they sprang; so that we ought to recognize, with some modern mystics and critics of the Church, the complete illegitimacy of any kind of attempt at agreement, corporate action or organization. The saying of Christ, " The wind bloweth where it listeth," is not to be pleaded in this connection. First of all, the text is in itself ambiguous; it is not clear whether it means the wind or the Spirit; if it is the wind, it seems a somewhat unscientific statement, and if it is the Spirit, while it is then perfectly true as a descrip-

THE HOLY SPIRIT AND THE CHURCH

tion of the spontaneity of His action, the consequences of His action are not to throw men apart in confusion, but to drive them together. Unless this is the ultimate result, we should either have to allow that God could be the author of confusion, or admit that individuals have failed to respond fully to the guidance of the Spirit. Indeed, if we take the modern signs of spiritual desire and response, of which fortunately there are many, but of which, unfortunately, the results are so slight; in so far as men remain in isolation or opposition to the Church, it cannot but be noticed how the sense of the Spirit in such souls becomes tenuous, the idea of Him impersonal, their experience fails to convey itself to others and so leaves no succession; while one is able to detect sometimes a purely selfish point of view, a claim to certainty and superiority of revelation without any recognition of the sources on which it really depends and the responsibility for seeing that it shall be conveyed to others and continued for ever. However imperfect as an instrument of the Spirit the Church may yet be, it is nevertheless within the Church that the movement of the Spirit persists, continually revives, makes reforms from within, and promises through it, and through it only, permanence and perfection.

Moreover, if humanity is ever to be the subject of redemption, this must include not only individual souls, but society, that is souls in their relationship one to another. Although organization has its limits, which must be recognized, if there is anything certain, it is that man cannot progress without co-operation, and therefore without agreement and organization. And if it had to be concluded that the Spirit of God was inevitably thwarted, quenched and destroyed merely by the human necessities of organization, then the redemption of man would have to be regarded as impossible; for individual souls, however spiritually great they may be, and in whatever isolation they may sometimes seem to emerge, can always be found to depend upon spiritual associations, inheritance, relationships. It is by their being gathered together into a body that the special endowments of individuals are the more freely circulated to others and their benefits conveyed to the future.

The relation of the Church to the movements of the Spirit in history may be likened to that of some great river which may occasionally overflow its banks, but which always shrinks again to the normal channel; and if it sometimes suffers loss through the divergence of a stream, that stream only loses itself and fails to find its way to the sea. Thus we may conclude that the highest work and ultimate aim of the Spirit of God is the formation of the Church, and that the purpose of the selection this may entail is not the exclusion of any soul from spiritual benefit, but rather the continuance all down history of an evergrowing stream, confined, if at all, only that it may reach the farthest shores of time and secure benefit for all humanity; and that it is this Spirit-created body which holds the promise one day of becoming the perfect instrument of the Spirit, the extension of the Incarnation, the very fulness of Him that filleth all in all.

II

THE APOSTOLIC CHURCH

IN the Constantinopolitan recension of the Nicene Creed it is confessed, "I believe one Holy, Catholic and Apostolic Church." It is with this last description of the Church as apostolic that we are at present to concern ourselves. By the Apostolic Church we might mean the Church as it was in the Apostolic age, and this would be identical with the Church as reflected in the New Testament documents; for we possess no authentic writings of the Apostles outside the New Testament, and if the Apostle John survived until the end of the century, then practically all the writings of the New Testament fall within the Apostolic age. But we do not propose to attempt any summary of the Church as reflected in the New Testament. In the first place this is unnecessary, because the documents are available and well known to all who are interested in the subject; and secondly, the New Testament documents, though all that we possess, give us only an occasional, incomplete, and therefore somewhat confusing picture of the Apostolic Church. This is only natural, for none of the writings sets out to give us a history of the Church, to describe its constitution, or to lay down its essential polity. It is this meagreness, and the difficulty of interpreting the material we possess, which have given rise to so much controversy concerning the authoritative constitution of the Church. Into that controversy we cannot go with any detail; the ground has already been microscopically explored, controversy has brought out every ambiguity and conflicting detail, and rival theories still contend for acceptance. For a full discussion the reader must be referred to works dealing more completely with the subject; we must be content to confine ourselves to general principles; but this perhaps with less loss, because it is probably through controversialists losing sight of general principles that the details have seemed beyond a comprehensive interpretation.

We shall find it is a good starting-point for our discussion if we ask what is broadly meant by the word "apostolic." An apostle means a person who is sent, or commissioned; therefore the Apostolic Church is the "commissioned Church"; so that when we declare that we believe in an Apostolic Church, we are confessing that we believe the Church has been divinely commissioned. We have previously seen that there is no contradiction between the idea of the Spirit's wide, unhindered action and the creation of an organization, both as a result of His action and as a means for making His action more effective upon the hearts of men. What we have now to inquire is, whether it is merely by an interior and spontaneous impulse that the Spirit gives the Church its divine commission, or whether the divine commission is conveyed through any external appointment and sustained succession. Is the divine commission a movement of the Spirit impelling every Christian believer to make known to men the message of Christ? Or did Christ Himself commission the Church by the appointment of any selected persons and by the endowment of them with an authority they are to hand on to others? Does the confession of the Church as Apostolic simply involve the belief that the Church is spiritually commissioned, or does it identify the Church as derived from the Apostles? By raising these questions we have set out the main points about which controversy has gathered, and their importance will immediately be discerned. For in the one case the Church's commission is interior, immanent in the whole body, and every Christian must be held responsible for the discharge of that commission, while in the other we shall be inclined to look to actual persons who have been specially commissioned and invested with peculiar authority.

Now if we look at the New Testament, first of all as a whole, we shall be compelled to reject the forcing of these alternatives as rigidly exclusive of one another; for it is on the face of it perfectly clear that the Spirit does possess the body as a whole, endows men with gifts, and moves them by an interior impulse to undertake different services; while at the same time it is equally clear that certain persons claim special authority and assume peculiar responsibility. The New Testament is apparently unconscious of any conflict between these two sets of facts; yet in controversy the one side has been emphasized to the exclusion of the other, so that we shall probably find it safest to keep in view both extremes. The one starts from a general impression, said to be derived from the New Testament, that spiritual freedom is everything and organization a matter of no concern; men exercise influence in the Church because they are endowed with spiritual gifts and not because they have an official position. Without staying now to inquire whether this is the whole of the truth about the Apostolic Church as reflected in the pages of the New Testament, let us leave this clouded and controverted area and move away from it until we reach a place where the other extreme is represented. We shall find that we have to proceed some distance down history, but we are at last confronted with a Church which

THE APOSTOLIC CHURCH

seems to be the very antithesis of the conception just outlined. Then we can work back and perhaps discern whether the change is due to a gradual corruption, a natural development, the preservation of an essential original principle, or the tightening up of an element at least present from the beginning.

We shall have to proceed as far as the end of the second century, and then we shall find ourselves faced by the distinct claim that the Apostles had left a succession, and that that succession is preserved by the bishops, whose ability to trace their appointment back to the Apostles constitutes their authority. For we find Tertullian, writing about A.D. 200, inviting the Gnostic teachers to produce their authority, which he demands shall be nothing else than the line of their bishops, going back to their first bishop, who "shall have had for his originator and predecessor one of the Apostles, or of the apostolic men who continued to the end in the Apostles' fellowship"; for this, he declares, is what Smyrna can do, for Polycarp was installed by John, and this is what Rome can do, for Clement was ordained by Peter. It is true that elsewhere Tertullian expresses quite another opinion. He says that the Church may consist of any number of persons who have "combined in this faith." This, he declares, will be the "Church of the Spirit," and it is this Church which will forgive sins by means of the spiritual men who compose it, "not the Church which consists of a number of bishops." This latter statement, however, was written after Tertullian had become a Montanist, and it only helps to throw into relief his earlier statement made while he was a Catholic. Now, was this later statement merely a change in Tertullian's preference, or was it prompted by an attempt to recover the original constitution of the Church? Tertullian does not

THE APOSTOLIC CHURCH

attempt to prove that Montanism is going back to the earlier freedom of the Church. Montanism made no such appeal; it rested its claims upon what it believed to be a further outpouring of the Spirit, which had made all previous arrangements unnecessary. If we now move back a little earlier than Tertullian, to Irenæus, writing about 180, we shall find the insistence upon the Apostolic succession maintained. He appeals to the "succession of the bishops," "who were appointed by the Apostles." True, he also speaks of the presbyters of the Church who have succession from the Apostles, and he sometimes calls the bishops also presbyters; a point to be noted. Justin Martyr, writing about the middle of the second century, does not refer to the question of succession, and in speaking of the Eucharist he refers only to the "president," to whom he gives no further title. When we move still farther back, to Ignatius, who was martyred probably in 115, we find him constantly insisting upon the office of the bishop, who, together with the presbyters and deacons, form a threefold order, without which "no Church has a title to the name." It should be noted that in the letters of Ignatius the bishop is a single official, and that he regards him as necessary to the whole order of the Church, the Eucharist not being valid unless it is under the bishop, or one to whom he shall have committed it. Ignatius does not actually refer to the succession of the bishop from the Apostles, but he ascribes to the bishop an authority that does not belong to the presbyters, making him the representative of Christ, while the presbyters are likened to the circle of the Twelve round the Master. When we come to the letter of Polycarp to the Philippians, written about the time of Ignatius' martyrdom, we find him calling upon them to obey the presbyters and deacons.

THE APOSTOLIC CHURCH

He makes no mention of a bishop, though there can be little doubt that Polycarp himself was the chief person in the Church at Smyrna, and Ignatius' letter to Smyrna involves the assumption that Polycarp was its bishop. The Didache is a curious document, and its date is in dispute, but it probably falls somewhere early in the second century. It refers to bishops and deacons, but it seems to give a much higher place to itinerant apostles, prophets, and teachers, who assume temporary authority on their appearance, especially in the conduct of worship, but who have to be tested lest they should be false prophets. When we come to Clement, who was writing from Rome to the Corinthian Church about the year 90, he declares that the Apostles knew that there would be "contention about the title of the episcopate," and therefore they appointed bishops and deacons, and subsequently gave additional injunctions that "if they fell asleep other approved men should succeed to their ministry." But apparently there is more than one bishop at Corinth, and they seem to be identical with the presbyters, although rulers are also referred to who may be distinct from presbyters. Clement nowhere refers to himself as a bishop, and there is no reason why he should, but he evidently stood in a position of supreme responsibility at Rome.

The general nature of this evidence is to show that, in this sub-apostolic age, it was generally believed that there were certain officials in the Church who derived their appointment ultimately from the Apostles; it came to be believed that the persons who marked this succession were the bishops. But although to Ignatius, and after him, this bishop was distinct from the presbyter, and the office was held by a single person, from the letters of Clement and Polycarp, as from the Didache, we should infer

THE APOSTOLIC CHURCH

that bishop and presbyter indicate the same office, although there are hints of some indeterminate persons who exercise superior authority.

If, with this evidence in mind, we now turn back to the New Testament, we shall note the following relevant facts. At the Church at Philippi there are two sets of officials, called bishops and deacons. When St. Paul meets with the presbyters of Ephesus, he calls them bishops; so that it seems clear that the two names were interchangeable. From the Acts of the Apostles we learn that the Apostle Paul ordained presbyters in every city; and from the Pastoral Epistles that Timothy had been ordained by the laying-on of the hands of St. Paul, as well as by the laying-on of the hands of the presbytery; and since Timothy is given instructions about the character of bishops and deacons, we should infer that, like Titus, he had been given authority to appoint presbyters.

Now the simplest way to interpret this evidence is to take the theories which have been put forward, and see if they do anything to clear up this confusing material. We may consider first the theory that originally the Church had no constitution laid down for it whatsoever; so that wherever men meet together in His name there the Church is constituted, and they can make what convenient arrangements they like, appointing their own officers, and especially the person who is to preside at the Eucharist. It must be admitted that on this theory room is left for the free movement of the Spirit, while nothing determines suitability for office but recognized spiritual gifts. But this theory can hardly claim to cover all the arrangements mentioned in the New Testament. It entirely ignores what was thought necessary according to the Acts of the Apostles; and, indeed, this theory can only claim to reproduce the original constitution of the Church if the authority of the Acts is laid aside as a later document, written with an ecclesiastical bias. For there the authority of the Apostles, the practice of the laying on of hands for the bestowal of the Holy Ghost, and the delegation of this authority to others as their representatives, are plainly set forth and obviously thought to be necessary. But this theory often appeals to the case of the Apostle Paul; for if one person can have a vision of Christ and feel himself thus sufficiently called and commissioned, that may happen again. And it may be pleaded that just as St. Paul had clearer vision, greater courage, and more abundant energy than the others, so persons directly called by Christ, and manifestly endowed by the Spirit, have arisen all down the ages to prove that the Spirit's unmediated selection is much more efficacious than any alleged apostolic succession. But this appeal to St. Paul assumes that the Apostle received no human ordination, in support of which his own emphatic repudiation can be quoted. But he certainly received the laying on of hands when he went forth from Antioch on his mission to the Gentiles; but while it is not certain that this was of the nature of an ordination, or that those that took part in it had themselves been ordained by the Apostles, and with power to ordain others, it is beyond doubt that St. Paul received baptism and the laying on of hands for the gift of the Holy Ghost immediately after his conversion, while he was recognized by the other Apostles and given the right hand of fellowship. Now, if St. Paul had cared to press his case to be an Apostle to the uttermost limit, he might have claimed that he neither needed to be baptized nor to receive the laying on of hands for the gift of the Holy Ghost, for we have no

THE APOSTOLIC CHURCH

record that the Twelve Apostles were ever baptized, and the gift of the Holy Spirit to them was not by the laying on of hands. The Apostles must be regarded as in a unique category, fully commissioned immediately by Christ's appointment and the gift of the Holy Ghost. But when it is taken into account that St. Paul was himself a great believer in order, that he appointed presbyters—which was not merely his idea, since presbyters already existed in the Church at Jerusalem—it seems more than likely that while his apostleship, as he himself rightly insists, was immediate from Christ, it was as necessary for him to be ordained as it was for him to be baptized and to receive the laying on of hands for the gift of the Holy Ghost. At any rate, it is quite clear that no one else can claim the status of the Apostle Paul, for that would not only mean claiming to be an Apostle, but one constituted so by an appearance of Christ of the same order as the Resurrection appearances to the eleven and to James, whose appointment, if he was not one of the original Apostles, must have been of the same character as that of St. Paul.

The second theory to be considered is that the Apostles left a distinct succession, but that this was of presbyters, who were alternatively called bishops, and possessed the power of ordaining others to their office. If this theory is true, it has to be explained how a single bishop arose, and how ordaining powers came to be restricted to him alone. One explanation suggested is that the bishop arose by means of an elevation of one of the presbyters to a superior but previously non-existent office, and that this was due to the influence of civic customs, combined with the usefulness of having a supreme officer around whom the faithful could be gathered when heresies and schisms arose. Jerome is sometimes quoted as holding the opinion that the episcopate had been thus developed by the election of one of their membership by the presbyters, which custom he declares had survived at Alexandria. But it is certain that Jerome believed that the bishop was distinguished from the presbyter in that he alone possessed the power of ordination; while if we are to make his evidence fit in with what we know from other sources was the actual custom at Alexandria, we must refer this action of the presbyters, not to ordination, but simply to election. A second suggestion to account for the emergence of the superior and single office of the bishop is that originally all presbyters were also bishops, and thus possessed the power of ordination, but that it was gradually found convenient to restrict the name and the power, first to a single person among the local presbyters, and, finally to an official who had diocesan rather than congregational attachment. On either explanation, it would be very questionable, on any theory of succession, whether presbyters had any right to resume ordaining powers, if at any time this had been taken from them. Apostolic succession through presbyters is, however, rarely pleaded; where ordaining powers are claimed for presbyters, it is generally on the theory that the Church has a right to restore what is held to be the New Testament practice. But it is exceedingly difficult to believe that such a restriction could ever have taken place without a resistance which would have left some mark, either in documents or in some Churches maintaining the older system even after the new had been adopted elsewhere.

An entirely different theory seems to be necessitated, and the only other one possible on the evidence seems to be that, first the Apostles, and then other persons to whom they specially committed the

THE APOSTOLIC CHURCH

particular function of conferring the gift of the Holy Ghost, were regarded as specially set apart and specially endowed by the Holy Spirit, and that such apostolic persons, other than the eleven themselves, are to be seen in Matthias, Paul, Barnabas, Silas, James the Lord's brother, and others; further, that distinguished evangelists and itinerant prophets were given these powers, and that eventually these were conveyed and restricted to persons who settled down in a city or exercised oversight over a number of congregations when the itinerant system came to an end. This theory would cover the position given to Titus and Timothy; it would allow for there being no such person settled at Philippi when Polycarp wrote to the Church there; and explain why these persons of apostolic authority were for a time called indiscriminately apostles, prophets, or evangelists, to whom only later was the name bishop transferred. For it must be remembered that functions must have been fixed long before names, which were originally only general names taken from elsewhere, and only later came to be identified with defined and restricted functions. The apparent confusion and the theories put forward are due to taking the same name as always describing the same function. The New Testament itself shows that this cannot be done, whether in the case of the name apostle, bishop, or presbyter.

If this explanation is rejected, then some other alternative must be produced, and this would only seem possible if resort is had to the theory that there has been a gradual development of organization and insistence upon official succession which has destroyed the earlier freedom of the Church and perverted the spiritual emphasis of the New Testament. But this theory will be forced to assume that this development has begun within the New

THE APOSTOLIC CHURCH

Testament itself. For if apostolic succession is to be challenged as a false idea, and episcopacy rejected as an illegitimate development, we must repudiate certain elements and whole books of the New Testament. The Pastoral Epistles, with their concern for organization and the delegation of St. Paul's authority to Timothy and Titus, must be dismissed as not only non-Pauline, but an endeavour to secure apostolic authority for an organization which can make no such claim. The Acts of the Apostles, with its concern for apostolic authority and succession, for the laying on of hands and official commission, must be dismissed as a later misrepresentation of the original conditions. Nor can appeal here be made to St. Paul's repudiation of human commission, his dismissal of James, Peter and John as only reputed pillars, and his defiance of Peter, as recorded in the Epistle to the Galatians; for this rests on a claim irrelevant to our question, presses language and a matter of disagreement too far, and is then faced with a St. Paul who himself claimed considerable authority over the Churches, has concern for their order, and must have at least recommended the appointment of bishops and deacons at Philippi. It is soon recognized that to make the theory of an originally completely free and unorganized Church possible, St. Paul must also be repudiated; and if this is done on the strength of an appeal to the Gospels, we must not only cut out the Church references in St. Matthew, and the commission contained in the closing verses, but the breathing of the Holy Spirit upon the Apostles and their investment with power to remit and retain sins found in what is often alleged to be the anti-ecclesiastical Gospel of St. John. It must be recognized also that it was the same person who penned the Gospel of St. Luke, which has no ecclesiastical reference, who writes the most ecclesiastical Acts; while the appointment of the Twelve must be deleted from the Gospel of St. Mark. And all this leaves us documents so discredited that nothing can be based on them at all. Moreover, every attempt to abandon the historic order of the Church and reproduce the New Testament polity is faced not only with a confusion, which cannot be made into a coherent system, because our records are incomplete, but with so many hints of fixed organization, special apostolic and delegated authority, that the later development provides the only clue which clears up the confusion and is the only possible system to adopt. It is far simpler to take our documents as they stand, and see in the later Church order of the sub-apostolic age a legitimate development of the natural concern to continue the Apostolic commission and authority of the Church.

The conclusion of the whole matter seems to be that the Church which would claim to be Apostolic must be able to show, first its Apostolic descent, and second that it has maintained the Apostolic order. And it seems much easier to believe that this Apostolic order depended chiefly upon a superintendent overseer, superior to the presbyter, and with wider than local authority, than that the episcopal distinction and function was a later growth. It seems obvious also from the consideration of fundamental principles that the Church must be a continuous body if it is to be a visible society at all. And since only the already existing society can admit others to its fellowship, this entails a continuous link with the original society, namely, the Apostles themselves. If this continuity is to be maintained, and if it is to be easily traceable, it is inevitable that the succession should be carried on through the chief officials of the Church. If it is objected that this subordinates a spiritual principle to a mechanical system, it must be pointed out that not only is it the function of the Church as a society to present the truth of Christ to men, and therefore continuity is needed, but it is the function of the Holy Spirit to redeem society, and therefore organization, and this particular organization claims to have been created by the Spirit. And since the succession is not hereditary, or limited to race or station, and can be combined with differing elective customs, everything will depend upon the gift of faith and the call of the Spirit to the individual, the Church only acting as the recognizing body and selecting this person and that to continue the succession and bear the chief responsibility of its commission. If the Spirit of God is unable to maintain such a succession as a truly spiritual instrument, then the redemption of the organization, and therefore of human society, is rendered hopeless.

But there is nothing in all this which demands that the Spirit never moves outside the Apostolic order or that no company of men gathered together to revive the Apostolic order outside the succession, or to construct some different order, cannot be an instrument of the Spirit or a witness for Christ. If it is difficult for any individual to plead the example of the Apostle Paul, as a sanction for starting a movement without the authority of the older society, there is sufficient in St. Paul's selection outside the Twelve to show that thus the Spirit of God may sometimes work, and even be compelled to work, in order to fulfil His purpose. Yet St. Paul was eventually recognized, and in some degree sought and was glad to be recognized by the original Apostles. Again, we have no indication who founded the Church at Rome; it certainly was in existence before St. Paul visited that city or St. Peter arrived there. And there is nothing to show that it was originally founded by an Apostolic person or that it had ever received an Apostolic delegation. Yet it is a trustworthy tradition that eventually St. Peter came there and was accepted as its natural head. Therefore, although there is freedom of development in the New Testament, there is no serious and permanent break with the Apostolic order. St. Paul is welcomed by the original Apostles as of the same standing as themselves; and St. Peter is accepted as head of the important, but apparently at one time leaderless, Church at Rome. There is no evidence in the New Testament to show what action would have been taken in the case of an individual claiming apostleship, and either not desiring or being refused recognition, or what would have been done with a Church refusing to recognize apostolic authority. There is, nevertheless, indication of how, alongside the Apostolic order, individuals might be in existence who were doing the work of God without apostolic recognition. We have an important example in the Gospels of the Apostles finding one who was casting out devils in the name of Christ and yet was not of their company, and our Lord explicitly commanded that he should not be forbidden. It should be noted that He neither condemned this person, nor did He abandon His plan of a commissioned Apostolate.

The conclusion seems to be that the Apostolic order should be preserved in perpetuity, but that it should be willing to extend recognition to movements of the Spirit that begin outside the Church, and to welcome those who are willing to be united with the Church, but that those who prefer to work in independence should not be forbidden or condemned. It is quite possible that if this toleration could be extended, while still maintaining the necessity for the official witness and the Apostolic order, there would be no permanent revolt from, or serious opposition to, the historic Church. It has been the making of the historic system rigidly exclusive which has driven men to the other extreme, and sometimes moved them to repudiate the system altogether. The maintenance of the succession, with toleration for all outside the succession, seems, therefore, to be the lesson to be gained from the Apostolic constitution of the Church. At the same time no Church can claim to be Apostolic which is not within the order and has not been recognized as in the succession; and there are now indications that a more spiritual view of the necessity for preserving the Apostolic order would suffice to bring together the scattered and rebellious movements into one fellowship again. Christ has other sheep that may not be in the Apostolic fold, but He cannot be content until He has brought them together into one flock.

III

THE CATHOLIC CHURCH

WHAT is meant when the Church is called Catholic? What further means of identifying the Church of Christ does the addition of this adjective provide? In attempting to answer this question we shall be plunged into a controversy that involves the whole of Church History, and is being carried on to-day in such volume and detail, and often with such prejudice and bitterness, that we might well be excused if we endeavoured to evade such a controversy; or finding ourselves surrounded by such a clamour of opposing cries, such a welter of obscure principles and impossible conclusions, we gave up the whole subject in despair, as beyond the possibility of rational decision. But this is an issue that cannot possibly be evaded, and we can only attempt to be objective, historical, and, applying the tests both of logic and of life, see what results we get. Detailed discussion, adequate historical references, the consideration of all ecclesiastical theories, are beyond our present purpose, and must be sought elsewhere; neither can we attempt to settle the question of individual loyalties; this must be left to personal conviction, the dictates of conscience, and the leading of the Spirit of God.

It would seem that early recensions of the Apostles' Creed expressed belief simply in the Holy Church. In the Constantinopolitan recension of the Nicene Creed the Church is defined by four adjectives, one of which is "Catholic," and it was probably from this example that the word "Catholic" came to

THE CATHOLIC CHURCH

be inserted in the Apostles' Creed towards the end of the fourth century.

What does "catholic" mean and imply? It is a Greek word, an adjective formed from two shorter words having the adverbial sense of "on the whole"; and it is employed to denote the universal or general, as opposed to the particular or peculiar. The word catholic continues to be used in that sense alongside the technical sense which grew up as it came to be applied specifically to the Church. The first record we possess of its application to the Church is found in the letter of Ignatius to Smyrna, written about A.D. 110: "where Jesus may be there is the Catholic Church." But it is not perfectly certain even from this statement what meaning the word actually carries. It does not seem to be used to distinguish the Catholic Church from some other kind of Church; it may simply mean that wherever Christ is present the whole Church is present.

Anyhow, it provides no means of identifying the Church, for the presence of Christ is obviously promised only to those who meet in His name; and who is to decide when these conditions are fulfilled? For defining the mystical nature and the plenipotentiary endowment of the Church it enunciates a valuable principle, showing that the Church does not depend upon either mathematical comprehension or elective representation. But for the purpose of identifying the Church it only involves enquiry in a circle: where Jesus is there is the Catholic Church; where two or three are gathered in His name Jesus is present; for in both cases the word "where" introduces an indeterminate contingency. Moreover, the statement of Ignatius has not yet been given in full, which is as follows: "Wheresoever the bishop shall appear, there let the people be, even as where Jesus may be there is the Catholic Church." In the light of other statements of Ignatius it is clear that he would define the properly constituted Church as dependent upon the bishop; this would thus be essential to any gathering that would claim to be " in His name "; the Catholic Church must be an episcopal Church; that is, an apostolically commissioned Church. When we come to about a century later we shall find Clement of Alexandria speaking as follows: " Both in substance and in seeming, both in origin and development, the primitive and the Catholic Church is the only one, agreeing, as it does, in the unity of the one faith." And now here it is obvious that " Catholic " has come to mean that Church which is descended from the original Church and is united by a universal faith. And from this time on one of the meanings of Catholic is that of orthodoxy as opposed to heresy; for now certain theories were making their appearance that were being rejected by the Church, and those who continued to hold them either left the Church or were actually excommunicated. " Catholic" therefore comes to be used as distinguished from sectarian; so that we get Cyril of Jerusalem, writing about 350, advising the faithful to " enquire not simply where the Lord's house is, for the sects of the profane also attempt to call their dens the house of the Lord . . . not merely where the Church is, but where is the Catholic Church." And the same writer also defines the meaning of the word " Catholic ": first, as diffused throughout the world; secondly, as teaching the whole faith; then as embracing all races; and finally, as healing all sin and encouraging all virtues. The word, therefore, still carries the meaning of universality, though not only of diffusion, but of aim, mission, and content. The Catholic Church is the whole

THE CATHOLIC CHURCH

Church, the original Church, the united Church, the orthodox Church, the universal Church, this last term having a moral as well as a geographical meaning. When we come to Augustine, we find in his controversy with the Donatists that this question of universality is still more emphatically stressed, for the Donatists were not, strictly speaking, heretics, they were only schismatics; that is, they separated themselves from the Church on a question of discipline, not of doctrine. But Augustine appeals to the fact that the Donatists are a local sect, and with them he contrasts the Church that is spread throughout the world. And he declares in words that sound startlingly germane to modern controversy, " whether they will it or not, heretics have to call the Catholic Church Catholic; although all heretics want to be styled Catholic, yet if anyone asks where is the Catholic place of worship, none of them would venture to point out his own conventicle."

Now this last quotation really brings us face to face with the centre of a still burning controversy; for there is one Church to-day that not only claims to be Catholic, but *the* Catholic Church, and even by common usage is generally conceded the name, namely, the Roman Church. It is this question of the exclusive identification of Christians in corporate communion with Rome as constituting the Catholic Church that we now have to consider. It is impossible for anyone to pretend to be impartial on this subject; but at least one can endeavour to be objective; and then we are bound to take note both of the Roman claim and of the fact that it is disputed. We must also ask those who dispute the Roman claim to be *the* Catholic Church what is their definition of Catholic. Various non-Roman definitions of Catholic must therefore be examined.

THE CATHOLIC CHURCH

There are first those who maintain that the Catholic Church is any Church that has maintained the Catholic faith and order. It is on this issue that the Eastern or Orthodox Church claims to be the true Church, and condemns the Roman Church for having added to the agreed faith at one point or another. The Orthodox Church, if we take its most authoritative declarations, would not, however, go so far as to declare that the Roman Communion was outside the Church. In the second place, the Anglican Church claims that its retention of the Catholic creeds and order entitles it to be called Catholic. But most Anglican exponents would admit that the Orthodox Church and the Roman Church were also Catholic, though out of communion with one another. And they would appeal for their standard of Catholic faith to the faith as defined by the first seven General Councils, and, in other matters, to those elements of faith held in common by those three " branches " of the Church. In the third place, we have to note those who would give the Catholic Church a wider circumference, and would include everyone who has been baptized. Fourthly, others would refuse to tie up membership in the Church with any external rite, and would identify the Catholic Church with all people in communion with any body which claims to be a Church of Christ, and accepts Christ as its sole spiritual head. Finally, others would make the circumference still wider in one direction, and identify the Catholic Church with all who call upon the name of the Lord Jesus ; while in another direction they would make it narrower, not necessarily including the baptized, or the enrolled and faithful members of any denomination, but simply those who are in vital spiritual communion with Christ inside and outside all the Churches, a number,

THE CATHOLIC CHURCH

therefore, known to God alone; not exactly an Invisible Church, since the persons are visible, but more strictly the Mystical Church, whose members cannot be with certainty identified by any external test or by the judgment of any human person.

Now, looking at these alternatives to the Roman claim one is bound to admit that they are all in one direction or another unsatisfactory. They have either to fall back upon a test of Catholicity which is archaic, static, and accidental, or to make it depend upon a rite like Baptism, which must include millions of people who have never been instructed in the Christian faith, have never themselves professed it, or have actually rejected and denied it. Again, if we are to include in the Catholic Church all corporate Christian communions, there is certainly no agreement as to where the qualifying line of Christian shall be drawn. For instance, does it include Unitarians or Christian Scientists, and many other smaller sects? The conception of the Catholic Church consisting only of the faithful known to Christ would be accepted by Roman Catholics as defining the Mystical Church and constituting the soul of the Church; but if taken alone it parts company with the correctness and visibility of the New Testament conception of the Church.

Therefore we are compelled to turn back and re-examine the Roman claims, and see if they are any more satisfactory. They are founded first of all upon the fact of unbroken historical descent: the Roman Church is directly descended from the primitive Church; no one disputes that. But so are other bodies which claim to be Churches, notably the Orthodox Church; and even the Lesser Eastern Churches, divided not only from the Roman, but from

THE CATHOLIC CHURCH

the Orthodox Church, and in heresy, can nevertheless claim direct descent from the primitive Church, as well as preserving the Apostolic order and succession. But Rome also claims that all other Churches, whether heretical bodies, the Eastern Orthodox, the Anglicans and other Reformation Churches, have broken away from her. It must be confessed that this is historically true. Moreover, an examination of the circumstances of the Great Schism, which took place in the eleventh century between the Eastern Church, which had its patriarchal head at Constantinople, and the Western Church, which had its head at Rome, shows that the Eastern Church did then repudiate a supremacy which it had been previously in the habit of conceding to the Roman Patriarchate. It takes two parties to make a quarrel, and even when a schism occurs, the responsibility for the schism need not rest wholly upon the body that actually tears itself away. But although Rome was not blameless, the actual as well as the formal responsibility does seem to rest the more heavily upon the Eastern Church. The actual schismatic act is even more clearly charged to those Churches which at the Reformation repudiated the Roman Church and deliberately separated themselves from its communion. For this there seemed to many earnest men only all too sufficient excuse. And it certainly looks as if Rome was more responsible for the Reformation Churches breaking away than for the Eastern Schism, for her supremacy had become secularized and her moral condition scandalous: though whether even that excuses schism must still be considered. But Rome does more than simply claim that the other Churches have broken away as it were from the parent body; she claims that by this act they have forsaken the rock on which the Church must be built, and are therefore no longer a part of the true Church, and strictly not Churches at all. For the Roman Church claims that it is in her, and in her alone, that the promise made by our Lord to St. Peter is vested. The basing of her claims on her succession to the Petrine supremacy involves a number of assumptions: (1) That the great text in St. Matthew's Gospel, "Thou art Peter, and on this rock will I build My Church," makes Peter, and not his confession, the rock; (2) that the peculiar position granted to St. Peter is also granted to his successors; (3) that the Bishop of Rome as Pope is the inheritor of the Petrine promise, and by virtue of his office continues to be the only rock on which the Church can be built.

Now we do not propose to dispute the interpretation of the New Testament text here involved. It is granted by many Protestant expositors that Peter himself is the rock, and not merely, though of course because of, his confession. It is also beyond all dispute that, although the conviction was a matter of growth, and due no doubt to the exigencies and circumstances of the times, in the early centuries of the Church, and from every part of the Church until the Great Schism, it was allowed that the Bishop of Rome was St. Peter's successor, that the Petrine See was the rock of the whole Church, and that Rome had a supremacy, a responsibility, and a promise attached to it higher than all other sees, even though they could claim direct Apostolic descent. Though there has been development, and this development has been due to natural causes, such as the fact that Rome was the Imperial Capital, there is nevertheless, if not a complete sanction, yet a prophecy of this in the promise made to St. Peter, and a partial recogni-

THE CATHOLIC CHURCH

tion of the position this gave to him is set forth in the leadership taken and accorded to him in the Acts of the Apostles. Moreover, there is a certain confirmation of the Roman claim in the appeal to the actual facts of history. The Roman Church has continued extraordinarily stable in doctrine. Despite some additions which she has made, such as in the Filioque clause, added to the Nicene Creed, the doctrines of the Immaculate Conception and the infallibility of the Pope, it will be admitted that she has never denied or gone back upon any part of the historic faith, even though her fidelity on this point might be regarded as due to a mere rigidity, motived by a prudential instinct and formal determination never to deny what has once been promulgated as of the essence of the faith. Again, in the great upheavals which have overtaken the world, and in the schisms that have overtaken the Church, the Roman Church has remained fundamentally unshaken, and has preserved a most extraordinary unity. Further, she has maintained the universal note of Catholicism in that she is not, like other Churches, such as the Anglican or the Greek, limited to nationality, tongue, or race, but is still the most universally diffused Church. All Churches are now conscious of their universal mission, and by the test of universal diffusion, Anglicans, Presbyterians, Methodists, and even the Salvation Army, might claim a quite respectable catholicity. But they were originally, and still remain, local in their colouring and outlook, and, by admission, sectarian; for the very unsectarianism which is now often boasted, in that some of these Churches will not invade another sphere, and others would not try to convert other denominations to their own, is a confession that they do not feel a universal mission; while

THE CATHOLIC CHURCH

the proselytizing of Rome, which is so sore a point with the other Churches, and looks so sectarian, is not only justified, but demanded, on her principles of the one Church with its universal mission. But these objective historic facts, and the logical position, are impressive, and this impression does not fail to register itself in the minds of many Protestants and of many outside the Christian faith altogether. There are few students of Church History who now go the length of denying that the Roman Communion does represent by history and unbroken descent the original Church. If some extreme Protestants might feel compelled to hold that Rome had actually fallen away, they would have to consider that this destroys the guarantee of any other Church never failing in the same way, and thus gives no permanence to Christianity, and negates the definite promise of Christ that the gates of hell shall not prevail against the Church. No respectable controversialist would now identify Rome with the Mystic Whore, or declare it to be the Church of antichrist; but while this marks an increase in charity, it only makes the issue more acute. For if Rome is not antichrist, what is she, if not what she claims to be? The abandoning of one identification demands the finding of another.

Thus if it is granted that Rome is a Church, are we compelled to go farther and accept her own claim that she is the only true Church of Christ, and that all outside her communion are not Churches at all; for since there is only one Church, and no other Church claims, or can support its claim, that it is the one Church, if we are to identify that one Church, where else save Rome are we to look? For if we say all the Churches constitute the one Church, they are not one, they do not all acknowledge one another, and each would draw the boundary line at a different place. Yet it is a little difficult to be certain what the Roman claim on this point actually is. It allows that some of the other Churches have maintained their Orders, and that their sacraments are therefore valid. There is probably no *de fide, ex cathedra* infallible statement which can be pointed to, in which the Roman Communion has laid down that it alone is the one and only Church of Jesus Christ here on earth; at any rate there has never been any proposal to insert the word Roman before the word Catholic in the Nicene Creed. The truth is that there are apparently two schools of interpretation in Rome itself. There are those who, while they would allow that there are Christians outside the Roman Church, hold there are no bodies outside the Roman Church which can be called Churches, and who would therefore hold that if people want to join the one true Church, they must enter the Roman Communion as individuals, so that any talk of negotiations with Christian bodies pretending to be Churches would be a betrayal of her own convictions. On the other hand there are those who would say that the Roman claim that she is the one true Church only means she is the one Church which has kept the true faith; and that it is not their business, and it is beyond the possibility of anyone to declare that other bodies have not true sacraments, even perhaps when their Orders may be in question; or that Christ is not their true head, and their members are not members of Him. They would only claim to know where the true Church *is*, and not to decide where it is not. Further, they all recognize that all true Christians belong to the soul of the Church, even though they cannot be said to belong to its body; and as far as salvation and Christ are concerned, the former is surely more important than the latter, even though the duty of belonging to the visible body is imperative upon all who feel able to decide where that body is to be found. Moreover, the Roman Church has negotiated with corporate bodies, and would certainly do so in the future, despite what some more intransigeant and exclusive Romans have maintained and apparently desire.

We are obviously faced with a tragic dilemma; for if we allow that the Roman Church is the only true Church, then we have to put outside the Church something approaching to half Christendom. And when we consider their claims of descent, the tenacity with which they have maintained themselves, even when cut off from communion with the rest of the Church, their saints and martyrs, their faith and works—despite temporary or local aberrations, the adoption of formal heresies which nevertheless do not make much actual difference to their devotion and fundamental spiritual orthodoxy —the logic that would decide that Rome was the only Church of Christ and the rest were not Churches at all, seems to involve a conclusion which is historically hopeless and ridiculous. Yet, on the other hand, if we are to allow Rome to be a true Church at all, then can we say that she has gone wrong or fallen into error, or that she is maintaining to-day an exclusive position which the true Church of Christ has not every right to maintain? There is a much deeper issue at stake than the claims of any one Church or the winning of any controversy. Just because the Roman Church makes such claims, if she then is wrong, it does look as if our Lord's promise to His Church has been completely broken. For just because Rome makes such high claims, if these are dismissed as false, then even less can other Churches claim to have inherited the promise

THE CATHOLIC CHURCH

of being the rock, of holding the keys, or of being led into all truth. How then can we escape this dilemma? If we admit the Roman claim, are we to deny any church standing to the other Churches? If we do not admit the Roman claim, we have to confess that the promise of Christ made to His Church is nowhere at present in fulfilment.

Looking at the history of the past, we have to recognize that the responsibility for schism and even the cause of heresy may have lain on the overpressing of authority on the part of the parent body, or the impatience and the misunderstood definitions of the orthodox. There is no need to stress the fact that the Roman Church has often been guilty of using worldly policy and worldly power, not only for backing up and enforcing her claims, but for cruel persecutions and most unchristian ends; for this would be allowed by many Romans. Again, there is a vast difference between the actual faith to which the Roman Church is committed and the popular understanding and practice of it which prevails in that Church; so that sometimes it looks as if there were greater fidelity to the faith, even as defined by Rome, outside than within. There is a narrower and a wider interpretation of Roman doctrine always possible, but it is the narrower that seems to be most widely held within, and is unfortunately that which is generally understood to be necessary outside the Roman Church. We say nothing of the failure of many of her representatives and those in the highest places, for our Lord taught us to expect this; but the impression the Church makes as a whole, and the character of the lower strata of her membership, have not only had the effect of keeping people out of the Roman Church, but out of any Church and outside of Christianity altogether. There has never been any reassuring repudiation of the legitimacy of persecution, and there has never been any authoritative admission that the Roman Church through its head and members has historic deeds to repent of, or has often manifested a spirit and policy which have caused many to stumble and lose faith in the Church. Moreover, many of the Churches outside, deficient, it may be admitted, in possessing any historically descended commission, an adequate rule of faith or sufficiently valid sacraments, have yet sufficiently manifested an ethical integrity, a devotional fervour, a social concern, that it would be blasphemy of the Holy Ghost to deny to be the work of Christ in their midst.

But do these considerations help us in any wise to resolve the dilemma? It can be suggested, and nothing more is proposed, that something like the following is worthy of consideration. The Roman Church can be admitted to be formally *the* Catholic Church, and that not only by descent, but also the Church that has formally preserved the historic order and the faith; but the Roman Church is this only as it were on formal issues and by a logical test; but while life is by no means denied to her, or even the sustained production of sanctity—to which subject we shall have to return at a later stage—she certainly has no exclusive possession of life or sanctity. There is no warrant in Scripture, and there is no proof in history, that merely being cut off from communion with the Petrine See cuts one off from the Church. And the responsibility for many of the schisms that have taken place, although deplorable and in a sense illegitimate and even sinful, must be charged to the Roman communion itself in great degree. But these schisms have carried with them not only life and grace, but actually notes of catholicity which were at least sounding very dim in Rome and were in danger of being completely lost. Spiritually, therefore, the Catholic Church is much more widely diffused than Rome, and indeed beyond the confines of any visible Church organization. Nevertheless we must also hold that wherever the form is held there also the Spirit will never entirely die; and that finally Spirit and form must be one. It is therefore possible to hold that one day the form which the Roman Church has preserved will be found capable of a much wider and more generous interpretation; that with that interpretation the other Churches will be brought into communion with Rome; that with the putting aside of temporal policy, of all attempt to lord it over the brethren, the historic claims of the Petrine See will be accepted by Christendom. But such a thing cannot come until the Roman Church has changed its spirit, not necessarily its form; interprets its doctrines more generously, Christianly and humanly; and especially brings out to the forefront these wider conceptions of the Catholic Church which are certainly to be found and taught by some of her expositors, and seem to have the greater sanction from her own actual *de fide* doctrines. Until that day arrives, those who cannot accept the claims of Rome to be exclusive, while yet they accept them to be exemplary, not only may remain outside, without spiritual schism or spiritual loss, but must remain outside; for they are only outside formally. Their exclusion is due to ignorance either on one side or the other. We can therefore hold that Rome is the true Church, but that all " orthodox believers and professors of the Catholic and Apostolic faith " really belong to her.

When the exclusive interpretation is abandoned,

for it is not *de fide*, it will be found that men will be the more willing to enter the Church which does not falsely and unrighteously count as outside the Church any true, faithful and loving Christian. Moreover, we can believe that our Lord's promise will yet be fulfilled, that the historical development of the Church will not have to reverse its progress, and even that it will be upon the rock of the Petrine See that the Church will finally be built; that when the Papal supremacy, and then the Papal infallibility, are interpreted, as they can be, in a Christian sense, true to the only type of supremacy which the New Testament recognizes and which St. Peter himself exercised, and with which indeed the greatest statements of the Papal claims can be found to agree, then Peter, having been converted, will be able to strengthen his brethren. And meantime, not only do all the Christians outside the Roman Communion really belong to the soul of the Church, but many outside Rome are more truly loyal to Rome and her *de fide* doctrines than many in Rome; they are not unorthodox or schismatic in heart, and they may actually be doing more to hasten the day when the whole Church shall be built, as Christ intended, upon the rock, than many actual members and many ardent defenders of the Roman Church. And we can take refuge for this position in the very great authority of Augustine himself when he wrote: "The divine providence often permits, through the turbulent seditions of the ignorant-minded, even good men to be driven out from the Christian congregation . . . those the Father who sees in secret, secretly crowns."

IV

THE HOLINESS OF THE CHURCH

IN endeavouring to expound the significance of belief in the "One, Holy, Catholic and Apostolic Church," and, first, in considering the meaning of the word "Apostolic," we have found ourselves driven to the conclusion that this entails identifying the Church with a visible and continuous society derived from the original society, which consisted, first of all, of the Apostles, and which has maintained their special office and commission. Although in Apostolic and sub-Apostolic times bishop and presbyter might describe the same person, we saw that it was not a question of name, but of function, and we concluded that the special Apostolic function is necessary for preserving the order and continuity of the Church, and that this function is discharged and continued only by Churches that have maintained the Episcopal succession. In the second place, we have come to the conclusion that the claim to be "The Catholic Church" must certainly be allowed pre-eminently to the existing Roman Communion, though we also decided that communions or denominations which have dispensed with the episcopal order, or have deliberately broken continuity with the Apostolic commission, are not therefore to be judged as outside the Church, or denied the grace and presence of Christ in their midst, even though their disorder may lead to certain deficiencies and endanger their continuance. In the same way we decided that such breaches in Catholic unity as have been due to rejection of the

THE HOLINESS OF THE CHURCH

decisions of Œcumenical Councils, as in the case of the Lesser Eastern Churches, or the still more marked repudiation with which the Reformed Churches began their career, although it prevents these Churches calling themselves " The Catholic Church," does not mean that they have parted with all the notes essential to Catholicity; in some cases they have retained them at least in greater purity than the historic Catholic Church, which the Roman Church claims alone to continue by its inheritance of the Petrine primacy, its unbroken succession and its vigilant sense and practical discharge of a universal commission. Whether such a double standard is necessary and can be maintained will have to be finally decided when we come to examine what is meant by the unity of the Church. But we must now apply another test of identification, namely that of holiness.

In considering the designation of the Church as "holy," we must ask what this involves as an actual description of the Church's moral and spiritual condition, and inquire whether this further description enables us to identify more certainly and clearly the true Church of Jesus Christ.

It would seem necessary to decide at the outset whether belief in the " Holy Church " (which was apparently the earliest form of this particular article in what afterwards became known as the Apostles' Creed) is to be regarded, like some objects of faith, as a belief in something which is invisible, and would therefore allow us to assume that the holiness of the Church is a fact only visible to faith and not necessarily something that can be subjected to an external test; or whether holiness is such an indisputable and indelible mark of the Church that to identify the Church of Christ we must not only ask whether it is Apostolic and Catholic, but also

THE HOLINESS OF THE CHURCH

whether it is Holy. It would be admitted by all, including Roman Catholic apologists, that the holiness of the Church must be as visible as its Apostolic order and as indisputable as its Catholic claim; indeed, on careful consideration all would probably admit that if the Church which could establish its claim to be Apostolic and Catholic were not holy, we should be presented with the perplexing conclusion that the continuous, historic body of Christ's Church had become corrupt and perverted. Many are willing to accept this conclusion, not only concerning the Roman Church, but are also willing to proceed to the assertion that, just in so far as a Church has relied upon Apostolic descent, and in the very measure in which it claims to be Catholic, has it become careless about holiness and actually lost any right to that distinction. Before we turn to examine the grounds for such an assertion, it would be well to consider the seriousness of such a conclusion, though that in itself must not prejudice our acceptance of it if no other course is open. For if the more any body can claim historic descent, the more such a body actually ceases to be holy, or in proportion as any body claims to be Catholic, by this much does it become complacent about any departure from holiness, then we should have to admit that there is something radically wrong with the notion of a continuous, visible society; and we should have to fall back upon the extreme Protestant notion that the Church of Christ is not a visible society at all, but is composed only of those individuals whose holy life and character evince their vital contact with Christ, and who may be independent of any historic continuity or corporate contact, but owe everything simply to their immediate relation to Jesus Christ. If we are forced to this conclusion, it involves the further conclusion

THE HOLINESS OF THE CHURCH

that Christ either could not have intended to found a visible society at all, or that He was wrong in thinking that such a society could be immune from moral corruption; when it would have to be admitted that Christianity contains no hope for the redemption of society and no guarantee of continuance. Such conclusions should make us hesitate to accept without further examination the assertion that holiness is found in inverse ratio to the preservation of the Apostolic succession or the claim to be Catholic; moreover, they ignore the bearing of such facts as that our Lord chose twelve Apostles, one of whom turned out to be a traitor, and that He retained him in the Apostolate when He knew that this was how he was going to turn out; while in the teaching of such parables as those of the dragnet and the field sown with tares Christ recognized that both good and bad would inevitably be included in His Church, and even deprecated any endeavour prematurely to root up the bad, lest some mistake should be made and the good should also be destroyed.

And yet we must face the assertion that the Church which claims to be Catholic has often presented in history an appearance of anything but holiness; not only because it has included unholy persons in its membership, and some of them have climbed to the highest office, but evil and wickedness have been so widespread as to give the general impression of prevailing corruption, while the corporate action of the Church, undertaken with deliberation and unanimity, has sometimes seemed to be inspired by anything but sanctified aims. It was because of abuses, scandals, worldly corruption and lax morality that the Reformers of the sixteenth century felt it to be a necessity to separate themselves vigorously and completely from the his-

THE HOLINESS OF THE CHURCH

toric Church; and it is admitted by many Roman Catholic writers that there was sufficient excuse for this action, even if they hold that the action itself was a mistake. It is difficult to know who in these matters is competent to be a judge. There would be little denial, however, that, for instance, in some countries the Catholic Church is in a low moral condition, and that in some of the Lesser Eastern Churches and in the Greek Orthodox Church morality has remained stagnant or has become mixed with much corruption. It was because the Church of England was willing to reckon the whole nation in its membership that the Free Churches in this country sprang into existence, demanding that a standard of religious experience and corresponding purity of life must be made a test of admission to the fellowship of the Church. Protestants and Free Churchmen are perhaps not themselves to be taken as final judges in a case to which they are a party, but it will be found that there is a strong impression amongst them, in the first place, that Protestants are morally superior to Catholics, and secondly, that Free Churchmen have a stronger sense of individual and social moral responsibility than that prevailing in the Established Church. In addition, all Churches need to be reminded that the world's opinion of the Church's holiness is not only critical, but convinced that neither in corporate action nor in individual life has the Church any right to contrast itself complacently with the condition of the world.

Moreover, it has to be remembered that, when the world passes judgment on the Church, it does not as a rule make much distinction between Catholic and Protestant or between Established and Free. It may be said that the world is no judge of holiness, and that the Church would

THE HOLINESS OF THE CHURCH

expect the world to be hostile, for this our Lord Himself predicted. It is a fact that in the world there can be found a sometimes unreasonable, a sometimes undoubtedly immoral, and sometimes an almost insane hatred of the Church; but it is a fact that the world's hatred is not always due to hostility to the holiness of the Church, but to indignation with its unholiness, on which it makes a pretence which is hypocritical, and claims a right to condemn which is intolerable. We must be very careful that, in endeavouring to come to a judgment which shall attempt to be impartial by at least listening to both sides, we are not led into making any comparison of the superiority of Catholicism or Protestantism depend upon a standard of material prosperity or physical cleanliness. Despite the surviving Jewish idea that prosperity is always a mark of God's favour, and the peculiarly modern conviction that cleanliness is next to godliness, neither of these standards can be accepted as a primary or determining test. It must be remembered also that the Churches which have a longer historic continuity are more liable to corruption than those which have had a more recent origin. It must also be recognized that the Free Churches, for instance, start off by weeding out their candidates by the demand for an assurance of conversion which necessarily involves some external evidence of that in life and character. Thus the Free Churches build up on a morally eclectic basis; whereas the Catholic Churches ask not for a man's assurance of conversion, but for a certification of his baptism and his confession of the Catholic faith; teaching indeed that his life must be in accordance therewith, but leaving that to his own conscience, and not demanding any other evidence of this than the absence of

THE HOLINESS OF THE CHURCH

open and scandalous sin. It may be that on this issue the Free and Evangelical Churches are right and the Established and Catholic Churches wrong, but that is a point we shall have to consider at some later stage. At present we are only concerned with actual results. If it is admitted by Roman Catholic writers that the Catholic Church was in a woefully corrupt state just before the Reformation, it will be admitted also by equally candid Protestant testimony that the Reformation did not immediately bring about a moral cleansing. In fact, if the Reformation had any immediate effect in that direction, it was probably rather in its reaction upon the old Catholic Church than upon the morality of the new Churches, and it had even less laudable effect on the morality of the people in general. Luther's admissions on this score are sufficient evidence for his own country, and the Tudor and the Stuart reigns perhaps provide enough for our own. We have indeed to await the verdict of time as to the moral level reached by Catholicism and Protestantism; but in one matter of common morality—namely that of sexual chastity, fidelity and restraint—the issue is already showing signs of a verdict not reassuring as to the tendency of Protestantism.

Now it is an invidious, and indeed a humanly impossible task to attempt any accurate judgment on this issue; we can only record what the accusers and defenders actually say, and take into account all alleged facts. It is an interesting fact that the Catholic Churches continually produce persons whom they call "saints"; and by that is meant not merely a virtuous character and a high degree of ethical integrity, but of a peculiarly radiant type and supernatural level, which not only marks such persons out as superlatively good, but makes their goodness attractive, powerful and infectious, and obviously due to divine grace. Without disputing that sometimes persons have been canonized by the Catholic Church whose saintliness was judged by prevailing ecclesiastical and monastic standards, or that other Churches have produced types marked by great moral astringency, a passion for social justice and unselfish philanthropic activity, it will probably be acknowledged, even by many Free Churchmen, that there is something in the Catholic saint which is undisputed by the world's judgment, which carries with it obvious signs of the supernatural and is not producible, at least in equal numbers or continuity, outside the Catholic system. In the non-Catholic Churches we may get a marked type of respectability, a high level of public devotion and great strength of character, but it is often hardly distinguishable from that which can be produced without any religion at all. The oft-repeated claim that ethical agnosticism can produce as high a type as religious faith is more plausible when the comparison is with the non-Catholic rather than with the Catholic type. Again, Roman Catholics often point out that it was in the most corrupt ages of the Church that saints were produced of extraordinary height and beauty, thus vindicating their method of not making a high ethical profession or attainment a condition of Church membership. And when we turn to the comparisons often made between the Church as a whole and the world, while not denying for a moment that non-religious persons often attain a very high standard of goodness, kindness and self-sacrifice, it is to be suspected, on the one hand, that they draw more than they know from Christian roots or unconfessed divine aid, and, on the other, that they are often unable to inspire goodness

THE HOLINESS OF THE CHURCH

in others, still less to convey the secret of their strength to the morally weak. It must be remembered also that the Church does not profess to consist of holy men or of strong men, but of men who desire to be holy and who, conscious of their weakness, turn for help to the grace which the Church can give. The Church really consists not of the holy, but of those who are being made holy: of penitent sinners who desire to be made saints. The issue is whether the Church possesses the power of welcoming into her ranks, on the confession of faith alone, the most unpromising and spoiled material, and yet is able to produce the most wonderful ethical and spiritual results; and whether the non-religious world can by any ethical exhortation, educational method or medical treatment, produce anything like such results. You might as well compare one hundred selected cases of persons living ordinary lives, whose lungs were in a perfectly healthy condition, with one hundred cases taken from a sanatorium: the question is, given infected lungs, does the ordinary life or the sanatorium produce the best results?

We have now to inquire, with these considerations in mind, in what sense the Church can be called holy, and how far the note of holiness enables us to determine the true Church. It must be remembered that the word " holiness " denotes not merely freedom from sin and the attainment of virtues: it describes a condition of a man's total personality which alone enables him to see God, to dwell for ever in His presence, and to become finally united to Him. There can be no possible dubiety that the attainment of holiness demands a very high ethical condition; but in its motive, in its eternal reference, and in its peculiar influence, holiness is to be distinguished from the ethical

THE HOLINESS OF THE CHURCH

substratum on which it has to rest. It is not a substitute for ethics; it claims in the end to produce the highest type of ethical attainment; but it is itself something more. In the pursuit of holiness ethical integrity is sought not to win the approval of men, or to attain a satisfying consistency of character, peace of conscience, or morality at all for its own sake, but in order that one may be fit to behold God and enjoy eternal life. Whether this is a worthy or the highest motive is, of course, a matter of dispute between the purely ethical and the religious person, and cannot be decided here. What religion claims is that, although the desire for holiness may be implanted long before high ethical integrity or correspondence and consistency of character have been attained, this aim and this motive will in the end produce a far higher type and, in addition, will have this value for humanity: that it will prove much more attractive than mere ethical righteousness, and it will be in the possession of a motive and a method which it can persuade others, even weak men and gross sinners, to adopt. The ethically righteous man may often be not only discouraging to his weaker and yet more struggling fellows, but be positively hateful to persons conscious of their sin and failings; whereas the saint is an encouragement to sinners and often the cause of their conversion.

Now the holiness of the Church consists, first of all, in its holy aim of bringing men to God; secondly, in its holy message, which publishes the eternal destiny of man and his capacity for union with God, proclaiming this as possible to all men of whatsoever type or ethical handicap; and thirdly, in its possession of the sanctifying grace which enables the greatest of sinners to become the greatest of saints. The Church believes that it

THE HOLINESS OF THE CHURCH

keeps alive in the world a much higher ethical standard, because it proclaims this destiny and offers this reward; that without it men would soon sink in large numbers to sheer bestiality, their highest attainments would remain mere respectability, while secular ethics would probably lead to the encouragement of merely social virtues which in the end would construct a social system which would be cruel, unprogressive, and finally destructive. The Church claims that its ethical value to the world rests primarily upon the nature of its holy gospel. It is not legitimate criticism to say that the Church encourages men to be ethical for the sake of an alien reward, for to offer the prize of union with God is simply to offer to men eternal communion with a Person who is ethically perfect and infinitely holy. In any true interpretation of the terms, the eternal reward of union with God is simply the maxim of "virtue is its own reward" *in excelsis*; only with wider horizons and an infinite character being given to virtue.

It is a lamentable fact that in the course of history persons have gained admission to the Church under the pretence, hypocritically false or due to self-deception, that they held the Church's faith and desired the gift of holiness, and who have maintained not only an inconsistent character, but lived scandalous lives. It is further admitted that some of these have climbed into positions of power, so that in some cases they have been the very persons specially entrusted with this message of holiness and with supreme responsibility for setting forth an example of sanctity in their own lives, and securing the purity of the Church by their conduct of its affairs. In contrast to all this, however, stands the life and witness of the saints, which more than outbalances the scandal that such

THE HOLINESS OF THE CHURCH

persons cause or the actual injury they have been able to do to the Church. This contrast holds good when we compare the Catholic with the Reformed Churches; for while it may perhaps be acknowledged that the Reformed Churches have preserved a higher general ethical level, and they have never tolerated such notorious evil livers as the Catholic Church has tolerated, it will perhaps also be admitted that they have never produced such saints: if they have never fallen so low, they have also never risen so high. The policy, therefore, of separating from the historic Church in order to secure the cleansing of the Church, however much it may have seemed justified in the eyes of those that did it, and under whatever sincere conviction and pain it was sometimes effected, defeated its own aim. It has re-introduced the peril of Pharisaism, with which the Reformed Churches have constantly been infected; it has failed to attain the same height of sanctity that has been attained even amidst the corruptions of the ancient Church; and the tracing of these corruptions to some doctrinal root or to some type of devotion has led the Reformed Churches to be careless about their theological basis and to diminish the practice of the devotional life, with serious consequences to their religious spirit; so that if there has been a welcome heightening of the general ethical level, there is also a disquieting tendency towards mere ethicism, which, because it parts with its inspiration, is bound at last to become hard, unbalanced and vulnerable to scepticism concerning these ethical values which Christianity alone has created and alone can conserve. And finally, the separation from the ancient Church has done nothing, save by indirect reaction, to purify that body itself, and has indeed subtracted from

THE HOLINESS OF THE CHURCH

it the very elements which might have brought about its cleansing. Moreover, everyone who claims still to belong in any sense to the Church has to bear the responsibility for the Church's failings in the past, and no amount of individual separation or denominational segregation can save us from that responsibility both in spiritual fact and in the judgment of the world.

It is when we come to the Church's corporate action that the test of sanctity seems to produce so little positive evidence of the presence of an active spirit of holiness within the Church. Ethical idealists outside the Church, looking back on Church history, want to know what evidence there is in such actions, say, as the Crusades or the Inquisition for the peculiar holiness of the Church; or in the Church's attitude towards, say, slavery, cruelty to animals, or military warfare, wherein it has not manifested a conscience on the level with that found in certain thinkers outside the Church, not to speak of being in advance of the general opinion of the world. And when modern apologists of the ancient Church refer to the general spirit of the age and ask that the Church's action should be judged only in the light of the general ethical level civilization had then reached, they only provoke the retort that the Church is supposed to lead mankind, to be far in advance of the ordinary conscience of the secularist and the worldling, and to possess in its own documents clear teaching on which it ought to have acted. In reply to this it can only be said that the Church has also provided many protests against acquiescence in these things, and that while in the application of Christian principles its corporate conscience and official action often seem to have been wanting, yet in its jealous guardianship of these documents and

THE HOLINESS OF THE CHURCH

its authoritative sanction of their teaching in the maintenance of man's supernatural destiny and the converting power of divine grace, the Church has preserved that inspiration for all social, humanitarian and philanthropic reforms, without which they would undoubtedly perish or pass into perversions. The application of the principles of Christianity runs out into such vast details, and is so far reaching in its ideals, that it is not fair to contrast persons or sects who seize upon one neglected or undiscerned point of Christian ethics, and make a speciality of that, with a Church that has to maintain both the root principle of divine revelation and its far-spread application to the whole of human life.

Nevertheless these considerations make it all the more necessary for us to maintain the kind of double position to which our conclusions have previously tended: that while the Catholic Church, in its narrowest definition, is both the root and core of Christianity, unless we are willing to recognize the marks of that holiness which should characterize the true Church, first of all in the Churches that are temporarily in division, through misunderstandings on both sides, and, then going further afield, in the reformers and idealists who, even when they have been in opposition to the Church and have themselves denied the Christian faith, have nevertheless stood for the things the Church ought to have been more alive to, we shall be unable to maintain either that the historic Catholic Church, or the totality of Christian denominations, fully deserve the title " holy." While, then, this test does not deny the conclusions which we have previously reached, as to where the core and centre of the Church is to be found, it does demand that the circle of the Church shall be drawn much wider,

THE HOLINESS OF THE CHURCH

not only than the Roman Church or the Churches claiming to be Catholic, or any bodies which claim to be Churches, but so as to include many who have no Church attachment whatsoever.

Nevertheless, we are equally convinced that the root and fount of holiness is, and will always remain, in the historic body that maintains the Apostolic order and is united within itself. But this body must be more prepared to receive and to consider criticisms of the world outside, to recognize that responsibility for schisms has often rested with the historic body, especially when traceable to its toleration of uncleanness and unholiness. If it would purge itself from all defilement, and save itself from being a reproach to the name of Christ, it must consider the safeguards which Protestantism may have made too hard or pushed too far, and make room for them within its more humane and tolerant system; and with acknowledgment of its own sins, it must seek reconciliation with its separated brethren, and confess openly and humbly to the world how it has misrepresented Christ to those who are without by its failure to follow Him in holiness of life.

Meantime, it can be claimed that the Church's holiness is a matter of progress towards an ever more exacting standard, and is a process which is bound to be gradual. But for those who are already members of any Christian communion, the method of sanctifying the Church must obviously not be attempted by separation, but rather by the example of a saintly life carried to heroic degree; the demand for the application of the Christian faith to any abuse or evil must be made within the Church, with patient persuasion as well as with prophetic zeal; and all Christian people should take upon themselves the priestly task of interceding

THE HOLINESS OF THE CHURCH

for the Church until our Lord's intention to " purify unto Himself a people, for His own possession, zealous of good works," and to " present the Church to Himself a glorious Church, not having spot or wrinkle or any such thing, but that it should be holy and without blemish," shall have been accomplished, not only sufficiently to silence the criticisms of the world, but even to satisfy His own holy purpose and exigent demand.

V

THE UNITY OF THE CHURCH

THE unity of the Church is its first characteristic mentioned in the Creed; we are asked to confess: I believe *One*, Holy, Catholic and Apostolic Church. These characteristics have been dealt with in inverse order; but this has been only for convenience, and must not be taken to imply that the unity of the Church is the least important; for if we may not say that unity is the most important note of the Church, it is certainly that which completes and harmonizes the rest. But when the question of unity is considered first it often comes to be applied too emphatically and to the exclusion of the other distinctive marks; for if we could simply decide at the outset that the Church which was united was the One True Church, then we should not have any need to discuss the other characteristics of Holiness, Catholicity or Apostolicity at all. Therefore it seems best to reverse the order mentioned in the Creed for the purposes of a more complete consideration, and to enable us to proceed from those notes which are more general to that which is most particular. It is at this point that we must face once again the claim of the Roman Communion to be the One True Church, for it is upon this issue of unity that Roman apologists insist so continually, and it is to this test that they appeal with such confidence of a triumphant success. It may perhaps be necessary to explain to some why any, or at least so much, notice should be taken of the Roman claims; for to many they appear

THE UNITY OF THE CHURCH

presumptuous, ridiculous and even blasphemous. To some they seem to involve a self-vindication which is, in the nature of the case, unbecoming, while the very spirit and confidence in which they are made arouse hostility and suspicion. For surely, it may be pleaded, a proud assurance and an exclusive claim were also characteristic of the Jewish Church, and only helped to secure its downfall. To others it seems ridiculous that one Church should make a claim which rules out half Christendom as altogether outside the Church, reduces the history of the past to unintelligible principles, and seems to shut the door of hope for the future. For it is constantly affirmed even by many who profess and call themselves Catholics, and are concerned for the unity of the Church, that, on the one hand, Rome will never alter its claims, and, on the other, that the other Churches will never submit to them. There are others, again, who regard these claims as blasphemous, because they feel they are so completely contradicted by the moral and spiritual condition of the Roman Church, both in the days of its ascendancy and in its present diminished position. They instance the resort to persecution, the use of political methods, the worldly ambitions and the tolerance of immorality in high places and of superstition among the masses. All these three classes would assert that the Roman Church has erred in matters of doctrine; an issue that we shall have to raise again when we come to consider the nature of authority. But we have already been forced to admit that, despite these criticisms, the claims of Rome demand serious consideration, backed up, as they are, by its undisputed historical derivation and undeviating continuity, its service and discharge of a universal mission, of which, among all the other Churches, it possesses the clearest consciousness, and which it has attempted to carry out by untiring efforts and zealous propagation; and since, despite so many appearances to the contrary, that Communion continues to put forth such unmistakable examples of sacrificial life and heroic holiness. We have given so much time, therefore, to consider the Roman claims, because, first of all, there is the fact that they are still being emphatically affirmed; secondly, that they have so much to support them; and thirdly, and most important, because if these claims are to be dismissed as valueless or can be completely contradicted by an appeal to historical and empirical facts, then we should be faced with the serious situation that the Church of Christ, in its most historic and continuous form, had become utterly corrupt and had fallen into irrecoverable error; when it would be difficult to see wherein the New Testament promises and expectations concerning the Church had not been sufficiently disproved by this conspicuous example as discredit Christianity altogether, and to show that the promise of Christ Himself had been broken or, at least, His power proved vain. Again, the simple dismissal of the Roman claims would leave us with no other sufficient embodiment or expression of Church consciousness, especially in its insistence that the Church of Christ must be one. It is not through any partisan bias, still less through any proselytizing purpose, that we have been compelled to return again and again to this subject, but because it is bound up with any serious interpretation of Christian principles and Church history.

It may be equally unintelligible, on the other hand, to some Roman apologists, why the Roman claims should not be accepted just as they stand, without further discussion, and as the only possible basis for understanding Christianity. But surely

THE UNITY OF THE CHURCH

there are few even among these who are without concern over the wider interests of Christendom, or who can consider the facts of the past and the condition of the present, and be content to dismiss the criticisms and objections that are raised in opposition to the Roman claims. The popular fears which are genuinely felt concerning the dangerous possibilities in admitting the Roman claims or in contemplating the re-ascendancy of that Church over Christendom cannot all be put down to mere ignorant prejudice or hostility to the truth; for that would surely be as blind and foolish as the contemptuous dismissal with which those on the other side sometimes seem to content themselves.

It can hardly be surprising that the Roman Communion should appeal to unity as such an essential mark of the Church, for it is the one most continually stressed in the New Testament: it was the subject of our Lord's latest prayer that His people should be one and in as close a unity as that which He possessed with the Father. St. Paul teaches us that, just as there is only one Spirit, one Lord and one God and Father of us all, so there is only one body, one faith and one hope of our calling. And elsewhere he shows that, although, as in the human body, there are different organs and members which have their differing function, yet this should not give rise to envy, exclusiveness or neglect, but " there should be no schism in the body." Therefore, it is argued, it should be perfectly easy to identify the true Church, for there can be only one. It is, of course, not sufficient for any body whatsoever to rise up and claim that it is that one; this must be substantiated. But defenders of the Roman claims can rightly ask where else we can seek the one Church when outside

THE UNITY OF THE CHURCH

the Roman Communion we are faced with a hopelessly confused situation, where numerous sects exist in a condition of division which approximates to individualistic anarchy. It can be pointed out that wherever any bodies have separated themselves from the historic body, that has only in turn provoked further schism and dissent amongst themselves. It is not possible to escape the logic of this situation by saying what of course any Church could say: Here are we who hold the truth, and outside there are nothing but swarming sects. For although there have been other Churches beside the Roman which have claimed to be the one true Church—notably the Greek Orthodox, the Presbyterians and the Plymouth Brethren, and at their origin many of the smaller sects—the logic of the situation has compelled the first two to diminish or abandon this claim, and in the last two cases the pretensions involved are so absurd that only an infinitesimal minority can profess them, while no one outside their ranks dreams of taking any notice of them whatsoever. Moreover, the Roman claim is not simply that here is the one Church, outside which there are only endless divisions; it claims not that it is merely the one contrasted with the many, but that there is only one Church that is at complete unity within itself; for here there is perfect unity both in faith and organization, contrasted with the others, who are torn by serious doctrinal quarrels, divided into national Churches, or each going its own way in order and worship, either by anarchy or general consent. For while in the Roman Church there is room for considerable free speculation and even warmly debated difference on unimportant subjects, the fundamentals of the faith may not be questioned, and while Uniat Churches are established which have their own liturgies and

THE UNITY OF THE CHURCH

continue their own customs, all are subject to the one supreme central authority. Neither can it be truly affirmed that the cause of all this sectarian division and individual confusion which has overtaken Christendom is due to the overpressing of conciliar authority or Papal autocracy, which has simply split the Church into fragments; because if that were true, then Protestantism, which is united in rejecting these claims, ought then to be itself united, whereas it is in the rejection of those claims that there is to be found its solitary bond of union; for the rest, there are not only almost endless differences of doctrine and organization, with a sliding scale which extends from comparative orthodoxy, episcopal government and complete sacramental observance to a dogmatic Unitarianism or even bare theism, to the rejection of all government, and no sacraments at all; but some of the most distinctive rallying-points within Protestantism—namely, Presbyterial government or evangelical experience—have, as in the case of the Presbyterian and the Methodist Churches, only given rise to numerous splits and divisions within those very systems, until it is only when we arrive at congregationally governed bodies, which demand complete freedom in matters both of organization and faith, that we arrive at an end of schism, because it may be said that schism has there been erected into a system.

On the other hand, it is nevertheless maintained that the unity of faith, the uniformity of worship and the centrality of organization attained in the Roman Communion is not what was intended by the unity outlined, exhorted and prayed for in the New Testament. And it would appear that there is considerable ground for this objection. After all, where is the spiritual value in a unity of faith

THE UNITY OF THE CHURCH

which is maintained by methods which hinder not only disloyal statement or free speculation, but even inquiry; or by the adoption of measures which seem to demand an immediate acceptance of what was only just previously a disputable point, with the only alternative of instant excommunication? It is easy enough to maintain unity of faith if, the moment there are the slightest signs of deviation or even the raising of discussion, the doubtful or objecting person is extruded. We are not at this moment questioning its necessity or discussing its expediency; we are simply pointing out that there is nothing supernatural in the results of a unity that follows from such methods. Again, if there have been any valuable discoveries or spiritual results in the forms of worship worked out in Protestantism, (and who would be prepared to deny it altogether?) then the uniformity of worship maintained in the Roman Church would seem to have resulted in depriving it of valuable means of devout expression and spiritual power. This subject of worship must be examined in more detail later; and we are not here asserting that the type of worship in the Roman Church, whether in its sacramental or liturgical forms, is in itself wrong, but that it seems exclusive of other forms which are also valuable and may be necessary.

Nevertheless, the alternative must be kept in mind. If the unity of faith and organization represented by the Roman Communion does not come up to the Christian standard, where else are we to look for it? Can it be maintained that outside there is anything corresponding to the unity which ought to characterize the Church of Christ? There can be found apologists even for this condition. There are those who propose that we should cease to lament over " our unhappy divisions " which,

THE UNITY OF THE CHURCH

because of their pleasing variety, they would prefer to call "happy" divisions; and others are so satisfied with the denominational divisions of Christianity that they regard reunion as not only impracticable, but undesirable. The denominations have sometimes been likened to the various units which go to comprise a fully-equipped army. This resemblance would be more striking if only these various units had not been so engaged in fighting one another and were all able to work together under a unified command. It is perfectly true that the variety in worship provided by the different denominations does appeal to differing temperaments, and thus would seem to provide, especially for our individualistic generation, opportunities for worship which, if they were lacking, might shut many out of worship altogether. But it also needs to be pointed out that the division into denominations for the purpose of providing certain forms of worship is a very doubtful experiment. We all have our individual preferences and dispositions, but most of us are brought up in families, in schools and in general society, where we have to learn to find some common ground; and surely the Christian Church, the Supreme Society, can plead a like necessity, and is actually intended partly to reduce, partly to provide for, and particularly to reconcile, temperamental differences. Moreover, there are a growing number of persons who find it exceedingly difficult to satisfy themselves with the exclusive forms of worship which the different denominations provide. They either want these different forms to satisfy different moods and needs, or they find they change with changing age and developing experience; and yet, if they want all at once, or pass from one type to another, they find this either prohibited, or the

THE UNITY OF THE CHURCH

passing from one to another a painful process. However, there are welcome signs that the hostility to Catholic worship is everywhere diminishing, however slowly, and forms and symbols once rejected are being re-adopted. No doubt the externals of Catholic ritual are sometimes retained and often introduced for purely æsthetic reasons, and sometimes in a fashion that leaves out the central reality that alone really sanctions them; so that the very Churches which have protested against ritual are really more liable to come under condemnation for sheer ritualism. But by one way and another, the experiment has proved the opposite that was sought, and the way is already preparing for a return to common worship.

If in the freest of the Free Churches the absence of exacted confessions or enforced creeds had produced nevertheless a striking and spontaneous agreement, and if the absence of legal organization promoted a real brotherhood between the Churches or an adequate financial support of the weak by the strong, and thus reproduced the kind of unity which existed in New Testament times, this alternative to the Roman method of securing unity would be much more impressive. Unfortunately, however, there have been only too many indications of a dangerous drifting away from the central realities of the Christian faith, and where this does not emerge into dogmatic heresy it often only escapes it by a vagueness which tends to become meaningless, and is becoming less and less adequate for the inquiring mind. At the same time it demands to be pointed out that, considering the divisions and the positive hostilities which have developed in the bodies which have separated themselves from the historic Church, there have been preserved, first, a most remarkable energy in reproduction and expansion, in piety and philanthropy; while if it is looked for with patience, and form is not made the only test, there has been retained what, in the circumstances, can only be recognized as a welcome, and indeed surprising, loyalty to the great central realities of the supremacy of Christ, and the power which comes from His Cross. The absence of a credal confession, and even a formal denial of some article of the Catholic faith, does not always mean that the loyalty of the heart does not remain. Ignorance and misunderstanding of Catholic doctrines, for which the blame may be not all on one side, but is often due to the popular interpretations and superstitious accretions found amongst Catholics, will account for much of the opposition which may be found. On the other hand, the acceptance of creeds and doctrines may often conceal insincerity, may be due to a wholly authoritative faith, which is not only ignorant, but tends to a misunderstanding of what is meant by any doctrine; so that one thing is professed but quite another meant, while the moral and social implications of the doctrine may not only not be perceived, but practically denied. These are considerations which have to be taken into account, so that too much should not be made on the one side of doctrinal disagreement, and on the other of credally uniform communions.

But there can be no doubt that, while all this should be recognized and given due weight, the confusing effect produced on the minds of men outside all the Churches, the waste of competition, and the prejudice and selfishness which sectarianism and denominationalism produce are beyond dispute; and the situation has become so desperate that attempts of all kinds and in every direction are being made to remedy it. The fissiparous movement of Protestantism is coming to an end, and

THE UNITY OF THE CHURCH

everywhere denominations are seeking reunion; at first, naturally, with those to whom they are more closely allied; but many are placing no limits as to the ultimate end of the reunion movement. Moreover, it is beyond dispute that not only is there an intellectual and spiritual revival taking place in the Roman Communion, but there is a constant drift from the other Churches towards that body; and, quite unexpectedly, because of their hitherto anti-Catholic, agnostic or naturally rebellious type of mind, distinguished persons make their submission to Rome, though sometimes that submission imparts as much as it receives.

The issue, however, remains, and is serious. If we admit the Roman claim to embody that unity which Christ willed His Church to have, then, on the one hand, it does not seem to be a particularly supernatural unity, as it is often obtained by such very natural, human and even military means; and, on the other hand, it not only condemns the rest of Christendom as being in the most grievous sin of schism, for it involves nothing less than rending the seamless robe and dismembering the sacred body, but it has to condemn the claims of others to belong to the Church of Christ at all to be a complete delusion and a ridiculous pretence. It would be difficult to reconcile such conditions with a sincere love of our Lord, any vital attachment to Him, or any susceptibility whatsoever to the guidance of the Holy Ghost: enemies of the Church of Christ may be bad enough, but pretenders to the Church of Christ would be far worse. No charitable extension of the doctrine of invincible ignorance will quite cover such a case; while the declaration that such are not counted by Christ in His flock, and are without His presence in their assemblies or His grace in their lives, would come perilously near sinning against the Holy Ghost. Yet if we are unwilling to accept the idea that the Roman unity fulfils what our Lord desired, and sufficiently answers to that which the New Testament demands (which seems to us quite impossible), then where are we to look for that unity which should mark the Church of Christ? We cannot see it sufficiently set forth in the totality of Christian denominations. Sometimes it is claimed that there is a unity of spirit which is all that is necessary, but this is really a confusion of terms; it is not unity of spirit that is mentioned in the New Testament, but unity of *the* Spirit, and that is expressly coupled with a corresponding unity of the body; where the one is recognized, the other is expected to be found. And no one can doubt that the unity of the body means something visibly harmonious and organic, and nobody can pretend that the present condition of Christendom represents any such unity. But, in addition, any underlying unity which may be claimed to be sufficient has, for all practical purposes, to except, first of all, those Churches which claim to be Catholic, and particularly the Roman Church, because they deny this unity to be sufficient and themselves exclude others from it. Agreement about this kind of unity would therefore be of value only if, for instance, the Roman Church were expressly repudiated as no Church at all, and this is a position which only a few of her most bitter opponents are now found prepared to take. Therefore no alternative expression of the Church's unity seems to be discernible apart from the Roman embodiment and idea of it; though another explanation does seem necessary.

For there is still another conclusion that remains open, and it is one which involves the admission that the Church is at present not united.

THE UNITY OF THE CHURCH

But then what becomes of this characteristic mark which the Church of Christ must show, and how is it any longer possible to confess belief in the one Church? Can we admit that the Church is not one, without surrendering a fundamental basis of faith? The situation is serious; and the conclusion may be more serious still. But we have already seen that in regard to the mark of holiness that mark is by no means perfectly possessed by the Church in its present condition; it is only set forth in its message and held up as an ideal standard towards which it is striving. May we not, therefore, assume that the unity of the Church may be an imperfect thing, and at any given moment not only fall short of absolute attainment, but may be temporarily broken? The New Testament certainly seems to admit the possibility of this by the fact, first, that we so often get exhortations to preserve unity, and secondly, that our Lord prayed so earnestly for it. If men have to be exhorted to maintain unity, it seems permissible to hold that there is a danger of its being broken; and our Lord would hardly have needed to pray for that which was guaranteed and inevitable. It is surely possible to hold that Christendom has been broken up by a quarrel, which is, however, obviously a family quarrel: there is still a discernible difference between the quarrel which the world has with the Church, and the quarrel which the Churches have between themselves. It is lamentably true that the quarrel has descended into a refusal to speak to one another, it has even developed into open hostility, and there is actual repudiation by the one of another's right to the family name; but nevertheless it *is* a family quarrel, though unfortunately family quarrels are often the worst.

But the situation is by no means hopeless, and

THE UNITY OF THE CHURCH

this interpretation seems indeed the only one that can make sense of the past or hold out hope for the future. It enables us to hold that there is still a unity preserved beyond all dissension in the very claim to be Christians, and in the desire to do the Lord's will, and submit to the monitions of the Divine Head of the Church. And this unity, while insufficient to satisfy the New Testament standard or to ensure our Lord's prayer, is sufficient to promise something better; for men on every side are now praying and seeking for reunion. It will hardly be denied by the best type of Roman apologist that the causes for schism are traceable, not only to impatience and rebellion in those that broke away, but also to the use of an authority which has no Christian sanction, the grasping at temporal power, the overlaying of the truth by superstition and the tolerance of immorality on the part of the Mother Church. And just as the Fall of man was foreseen and permitted by God, because of the greater mercy it would reveal and the even more wonderful redemption that it would make possible, so we may understand why God has permitted the unity of the Church to be broken, yet not beyond repair; and His grace may make it the means of finally securing a unity that shall be richer, freer and more Christian than had ever been attained before.

The breach of Church unity has been an incident necessary for its perfecting, and we may yet have good hope of a unity which shall rest upon loyalty rather than legality; which shall be freely rendered rather than autocratically enforced, and which shall be kept by the Spirit and not by the bondage of the letter. It is not beyond conception how this unity will actually be attained. Despite many setbacks and disappointments, despite inadequate

THE UNITY OF THE CHURCH

motives, insufficient principles, and despite the opposition that comes from exclusiveness or contentment, the work of reunion will obviously go on; denominations which have the more recently broken apart from one another and which have the more natural affinities will gradually draw together. We may look for a centralizing movement within Protestantism which shall by no means merely harden into anti-Catholic opposition; for we have not only seen Catholic practices and principles adopted by the Church of England which, at any rate, once was much more careless about them; but a similar tendency is invading the Lutheran Church, and, in one form or another, and although often without recognized principle, yet none the less surely, is growing within the Free Churches of this country and America. Some defenders of the Roman claims seem both to fear and to hate this movement; some are content to ridicule its lack of clear principle, its pathetic confusions and general ineffectiveness, and some confidently predict that reunion will never come this way. They maintain that unity must be sought by individuals, who are outside the Church, coming to realize their condition, and, one by one, submitting to the Roman claims. But there are other counsels, and wider hopes, and historic decisions which have been taken on the part of the Roman Church to which we can appeal; and it is not beyond conception that, despite the hostility to some Roman doctrines and the more widespread hostility to dogma in any form, and especially the opposition to Papal supremacy and infallibility, these doctrines may be so interpreted, and so understood, as to become finally acceptable. On the other hand, the necessity for dogma and the individual attitude towards it may come to be defined and allowed with more consideration of the

THE UNITY OF THE CHURCH

actual spiritual issues involved on both sides. It is quite possible for Papal supremacy and Papal infallibility to be interpreted in such a way that it may be seen to be the only possible fulfilment of our Lord's promise to build the Church upon Peter and his confession of His Christhood and divine Sonship. All this might take place without the actual alteration of a single dogma to which the Roman Church has pledged itself; though many might require a further explanation or a more liberal interpretation, which, by their nature, these dogmas themselves demand. It is not so much the dethroning of the sacraments from their present position as a more adequate teaching concerning them, and the corollary necessity of an interior life and a social application that is needed; it is not the exaltation of the Mass as the highest form of worship that has to be altered, but the provision of other kinds of worship, and other forms of devotion, which would only prepare the way for a fuller understanding of what the Mass means. These may be only supernatural hopes and perhaps prophetic predictions of still far-off days, but they alone seem adequate to answer our Lord's last and greatest prayer, gather up the lessons that must be learned from the past, and give a guarantee to those hopes which the Spirit of God Himself has bidden us hold concerning the days that are yet to come.

VI

AUTHORITY

THE Catholic system of thought and the Catholic conception of the Church make much of authority, whereas the general tendency of Protestantism is to diminish the place given to authority, and even to repudiate the idea as an alien intrusion into the realm of religion. It is felt by many disputants on both sides that it is this question of authority, and not so much that of ecclesiastical order or sacramental worship, which constitutes the real cleavage between Catholicism and Protestantism. But the extreme divergence into which the issue has developed will be found to be more apparent than real; for the most exalted conception of ecclesiastical authority has to rest itself finally on personal judgment; while, on the other hand, those who claim personal experience to be their only authority would have to own that in some degree their experience rested on the authority of something outside themselves. Again, much of the revolt against authority is due not so much to the nature of authority, for in some degree it is necessary and inescapable, as to authority having been pressed beyond its legitimate sphere. But the evasion, intractability and confusion which seem to attend all discussions on the subject are largely traceable to the wide content which the word has come to hold; different and yet inter-dependent things being described under the one term, which cross one another in argument

AUTHORITY

and thus confuse the issue. We can probably do little more with this difficult subject than attempt to clear away the possible causes of confusion incident to the different uses of the term "authority"; for there are discernible at least three distinct meanings of the word.

In the first place, there is the authority of *order*: we are accustomed to this application of the term when, in connection with public affairs, we speak of a "properly constituted authority," which means that some person has been duly appointed to act as a representative of the State. We have seen that in the Church there has been from earliest times a recognized constitution, and that certain officers, in particular, bishops in ordaining, and presbyters in the celebration of the Eucharist, are empowered to act on behalf of the Church as a whole. It would be admitted by all that any society has the right to order itself and to make its own rules, and therefore, it is argued, the Church has an equivalent right. So it is generally supposed that those who are in rebellion against ecclesiastical authority have failed to grasp the social character of Christianity; whereas the appeal from the analogy of a human society to the divine society of the Church needs careful examination. For it is conceivable that the nature of authority in a divine society might be different from that of a purely human society. Moreover, when the authority of any secular society is challenged an appeal has to be made, in the first instance, to the will of the majority, and, especially in the case of the State, finally to the power of the majority to impose its will upon others. There have been many attempts to reorganize the Church on a purely democratic basis, but it is doubtful if even the

AUTHORITY

most democratically organized communion would claim that a majority decision necessarily settled any point at issue, especially in matters of doctrine. It will generally be found that the more democratic, in the popular sense of the word, a Church becomes, the less it is inclined to claim any particular divine inspiration or authority for its decisions. Strangely enough, it is the most autocratic of communions that has claimed infallibility for its supreme head when making an *ex cathedra* utterance. In the case of the Church it is now generally agreed that the attempt to use force, and especially to invoke the power of the sword, is a mistake, and not only confuses the issue, but in the end always brings the Church under the domination of the secular power. Therefore, while we may admit that the Church as a society may have its properly constituted authority, it would also be generally admitted that the constitution of the Church has been laid down for it in the Scriptures, and although there is a dispute as to what the form of the constitution is that is there laid down, or whether it has there taken a final character, it would be agreed that nothing *contrary* to the Scripture should be included in the constitution of the Church. While, therefore, some kind of ordered authority is recognized, an appeal can always be made to the Scripture; and to that point we shall have to return.

Under this heading of the authority of order, we may also consider the question of authoritative teaching. Here again this use of the term is found in secular affairs. A statement is sometimes issued "by authority," or is said to be authoritative; and this means that it can be taken for certain that it is not just someone's private opinion, but it has been agreed upon by the properly constituted

AUTHORITY

authority. It is only natural that it should have been found both convenient and necessary in the Church for it to be ascertainable what teaching carries with it the imprimatur of the Church and what remains open to speculation or can only claim to be individual opinion. It is quite evident that from the earliest days some questions were regarded as beyond discussion within the Church. The confession that Jesus was the Christ was the foundation of the Church's creed; and out of this there has gradually developed a body of doctrine which can be taken to be held by the Church as a whole. There is almost no body of Christians which would not accept the idea there is some minimum of authoritative teaching; for if any body of professing Christians were to deny, for instance, that Jesus was the Christ, they would by that denial obviously put themselves outside the Christian Church altogether. But beyond some such simple minimum of agreed teaching very different standards are found. The Roman Communion can point to a very definite body of doctrine which can be declared to be authoritative; a body like the Anglican Communion is content to get on with a much smaller body of doctrine, namely that contained in the three Creeds, together with subsidiary and not completely authoritative formularies; while the Free Churches content themselves with more general statements of faith, and in some cases these are regarded as only indicative of what is generally held. In the present state of thought differently constituted minds seem to demand different degrees of authoritative teaching: some persons would even desire more than Rome lays down, and would obviously like a dogmatic ruling on every question raised; others glory in the greater freedom of speculation and individual opinion on the basis of

AUTHORITY

a very small area of authoritative teaching; while others prefer not only a general diffusion of vague ideas, but a constantly fluid and changing opinion. Yet while it is everywhere a matter of degree, everyone subscribes in some sense to the need for it being possible to declare that this is what the whole Church holds. Now, while this authority of order is in the main a question of convenience, any disagreement with it raises the question whence the Church derives its authority. The questioning of the authority of order, therefore, only brings to light another sense in which the term is used, namely the authority of *right*.

The authority of *right* raises one of the profoundest and yet most elusive of questions which the human mind can attempt, for it stands over against the more secular conception of the authority of might. It may be that in any human society the majority has the power to coerce the minority, but the question may still be raised whether it has the right to do so. It is of the very genius of Christianity to elevate the authority of right above the authority of might; but this only raises the question of how the right can be decided or whence it is obtained. When our Lord Himself was asked by what authority He cleansed the Temple, He refused to satisfy His questioners, and only asked them in turn why they recognized the authority of John the Baptist. He seems to have appealed, therefore, to a certain prophetic power which the common people were able to recognize. Moreover, on another occasion He exclaimed: "Why even of yourselves judge ye not what is right?" The Church is therefore unable to do otherwise than her Lord; and although the historic Church claims to possess an authority to rule her own household and to teach men the truth of God, even the

AUTHORITY

most rigid presentation of the Roman claims and the most dogmatic position that has ever been held always makes some appeal beyond itself; and that appeal is in the first place generally to the Scriptures. In the Catholic system it is generally agreed that, while the Scriptures must be interpreted according to the general mind of the Church, the sanction for the authority that the Church claims can be found in the Scriptures by the ordinary reader. And even when the Roman Church holds that those in communion with herself alone constitute the one true Church, no one is asked to accept this merely because it is so stated, but an appeal is made to Scripture and history, of which the individual must appraise the value. But here two very difficult questions emerge. In the first place, the Reformers challenged the right of the historic Church, because they declared that the Scriptures, to which the Church appealed, did not sanction much of her authority, her order and her teaching. For a time the appeal was, as has often been pointed out, from an infallible Church to an infallible Scripture; but it is more than interesting to notice that over a large area of Protestantism the infallibility of the Scriptures has been surrendered. Criticism has compelled a shifting of the ground, in turn, from the authority of the Old Testament to the authority of the New; from the Epistles to the Gospels; from the Gospels to the teaching of Christ; from the whole of the teaching ascribed to Christ to a certain residuum which criticism would regard as historic; and even within that residuum to a certain set of purely religious ideas on which alone is Jesus to be regarded as authoritative. At every point of retrogressive appeal there is wide disagreement among various types of critics, and the final authority of Christ is not only narrowed down to a very minute area, but

AUTHORITY

itself becomes vague and is on the point of vanishing away. In the second place, many who are inclined to grant more authority to the Scriptures claim that neither by their nature nor by their intention do they actually prescribe a constitution for the Church or lay down anything in the nature of dogma; and therefore, if they believe that either is necessary, they have to look to the authority of the living Church to determine them. In the third place, those Protestants who still regard the Scriptures as infallible, and then appeal to them in order to repudiate the claims or teaching of the Catholic Church, find themselves in serious difficulty. They have to posit an infallible selection of the component parts of Scripture, and the body which made that selection was certainly the Church. They therefore have to admit their dependence upon an authority which, on other grounds, they challenge; though it might still be argued that the Church exercised her authority rightly in her choice of the Scriptures, whereas the Scriptures do not allow certain extensions of that authority which the Church has claimed. But the actual circumstances of the case prevent this easy solution; for it is precisely amongst those Protestants who accept the infallibility of the Scriptures, while they deny the present authority of the Church, that the wildest confusion reigns. For while on the basis of the infallibility of the Scriptures the orthodox accept such doctrines as the Trinity, the divinity of Christ, or the immortality of the soul, considerable numbers can be met with who deny all three on the same Scriptural basis. Some reasonable conception of a living authority seems therefore essential to the preservation of Christianity or to the existence of any body which can be identified as the Church of Christ. But in the main these two meanings of

AUTHORITY

the word "authority"—that of order and right—raise only practical questions. Another question is now seen looming large behind them both: it is the question of the authority of *Truth*.

It will be admitted that truth has supreme authority, but the problem is to determine what constitutes truth. We begin this inquiry by noticing that in modern discussions concerning the nature of faith, which is necessary to discern the things of God, defenders of the Roman position are inclined to state that faith is belief on the authority of someone else; and this authority, it is assumed, must be the Church. The only Church which claims infallible authority is the Roman Church, and therefore faith must rest on the authority of the Roman Church. It seems a reasonable Protestant objection to this, that faith in the New Testament is surely something more than belief merely on the authority of another, for it is there stated to be the gift of God: a point which is specially stressed by Roman theologians. If faith were mere belief on the authority of another it would not contain in itself anything converting. Even if we could be absolutely certain that something had been declared to be true by the very lips of God, and it was believed on that basis, it is questionable if that could be designated as faith; the devils believe, and on just such a basis. With real faith there must be not only the acceptance of certain things as true, but faith must become a power in the mind and life. It may be perfectly true that all faith must eventually rest upon some authority, but it is not that mere fact that constitutes the sole distinction of faith.

It may be claimed that the repudiation of the Church's authority has only landed religious thought in an impossible position. We have seen that

AUTHORITY

criticism has been compelled to abandon the sufficient authority of Scripture and has moved back, in the one direction to a negative rationalism, and in the other to an appeal to religious experience. Nevertheless, the appeal to reason still conceals a recession to some basis of authority; it has to concede that reason is trustworthy, and this, in the end, means that the source of reason has to be trusted. And if the source of reason is not a perfect omniscient Mind there can be no such trust. Thus the rationalist rests eventually on authority, and on the authority of God. If we turn to religious experience, we are again depending upon the authority of God, but now as manifested in a certain experience which has a more subjective appeal than reason. If this is the retreat to which Protestantism is now being driven, it does not at the present promise a very permanent foothold. A genuine experience of God must be granted to many persons outside Christianity altogether, and it surely must be granted to many persons, for instance, who are members of the Roman Catholic Church. The appeal to religious experience would therefore validate every sincere religion. But in some quarters the appeal to experience would rather *in*validate all religion; for many exponents of modern psychology would regard religious experience as a phantasy or a mere transjection of one's own personality.

Over against this continual movement and final collapse of the recessive appeal to authority, the claims of the Catholic Church naturally present an alluring contrast. And yet before the authority of that Church can be accepted, it must be examined, and mere belief on the authority of the Church, even in Roman Catholic theology, would hardly constitute a sufficient faith. Religion

AUTHORITY

is too serious a business for anyone simply to say: "I believe the Scriptures because the Church declares them to be true"; "I believe in Christ because the Scriptures tell me that He was the Son of God," and "I believe in God because Christ tells me that God is His Father." This would make everything finally dependent upon the authority of the Church. But as a matter of fact even the Roman Church does not ask us to believe in her on her own authority, but on the authority of the Scriptures. Thus the Church seems to get her authority from the Scriptures, and yet, as we have seen before, the Scriptures get their authority from the Church. But the argument is not really the vicious circle that it appears to be. What is meant is that there is a coincidence between the promise of the Scriptures and the claim of their fulfilment by the Church. Moreover, Catholic theology teaches us that man comes to believe in God through the exercise of his reason; asking what is the cause of the world he sees outside him, he is driven to the belief in God. From that he argues that God would be likely to make Himself further known to men; and then he finds the Scriptures making a claim to such a revelation, culminating in the Incarnation of the Son of God. Again it is a question of coincidence, this time between reason and Scripture. Neither does Catholic theology omit to face the question as to the trustworthiness of human reason to decide the great concerns of fundamental truth. It points out the fact that we cannot deny the competence of human reason to arrive at truth, for to do so would be to involve ourselves in the contradiction of both affirming and denying a thing to be true in the same breath. On the other hand, it does not dogmatically affirm the contrary:

AUTHORITY

namely, that the human mind *is* competent to arrive at truth; but only asks that this should be accepted as a reasonable hypothesis and then see how it works out. Now if we are to accept the trustworthiness of reason, as we are compelled to do, the only confirmation of the reasonableness of that compulsion is the assumption that God made the human mind. For if the human mind does not derive its authority from Absolute Mind, then it either comes from some inferior mind, which must rest upon some other and unknown authority, or it comes from the mere evolution of mindless matter, when there would be no reason for trusting it at all. Finally, then, we rest upon the trustworthiness of reason as actually involving the authority of its Author; and yet we have to admit it is nothing more than a hypothesis, though withal an inevitable one, to which we are absolutely shut up. Yet everything does not rest on this alone. For when we look outside ourselves to the world around, reason, working by the law of causality, arrives at the idea of God. We might expect that this God would make Himself further known, beyond the disclosure of His power and mind in the vastness and order of the universe; we might expect that He would speak to men in their own tongue; and then we meet with those who actually claim to speak in the name of God, in short, the prophets of humanity. But we are now faced with a variety of prophets, though only in the Old Testament do we find a succession of such who claim to speak in the name of God, and who declare certain things about His character with great unanimity. Over against them there certainly stand the so-called false prophets, but they are distinguishable by their lack of unanimity and by their prophesying smooth things, obviously designed

AUTHORITY

merely to please people; there is an absence of appeal to the supernatural about them; they are confused and they die out. The Prophets' declarations are therefore confirmatory of what reason has already reached. But the Prophets' declarations themselves lead us to expect still further revelation, and this indeed the Prophets themselves actually promise, namely the revelation of God in person. Then comes Christ, who claims to be the Son of God, and here again nobody else has ever claimed to be the Son of God so emphatically and in so unique a sense, while at the same time fulfilling ancient promises, and having His claims accepted by those who stood nearest to Him. Once again, in turn, Christ promises to build a Church. And we have the Catholic Church claiming to be that Church, and finally, no Church but the Roman Church claiming that so emphatically and claiming infallibility.

Now it is not really the case that one authority rests upon another, until we get a final authority resting upon a pure though inevitable assumption. It is rather the case that reason, Scripture, Christ and the Church agree together and confirm one another. But even these are not conclusive until there has been a religious experience. These coincident authorities proclaim to the mind what is, almost beyond dispute, the strongest possible confirmation, but they are still lacking in something most important, namely that faith which brings religious experience; and it is this that now has to be sought, namely a supernatural conviction which produces a great change of mind and soul, the confidence of faith. Here, then, we distinguish that faith does rest upon authority, but it is not merely authority: authority confronts the mind, the mind is driven in response to seek for faith,

AUTHORITY

and faith confirms the authority. If this be a true account of the relation of authority and faith, we do not have a retrogression back to some assumed, but still very hypothetical, authority; we do not have an argument in a vicious circle; everything is not made to rest simply upon the authority of the Church; but rather we have a system of confirming authorities. Moreover, it can be claimed that this gives us neither a merely objective nor a merely subjective authority, but the joining of the two together in a mutual confirmation.

It is now possible to see what has gone wrong with the popular conception, as well as the widespread rejection, of authority: there has been an overpressing of authority beyond what it is able to bear. But this is not to be found in the true Catholic system, but rather, in the first instance, in popular misrepresentations of it, which have consequently brought about the rejection of authority. The authority of that initial assumption which we have to make, that the human mind is capable of truth, is not pressed into absolute certainty, but waits confirmation. Reason is not therefore exalted into that absolute place given it by rationalism, which in the end only destroys trust in reason; first because reason alone produces so many disagreements, and secondly reason obviously must rest upon something beyond itself; which rationalism, refusing to admit, only makes reason irrational. This error works itself out, so that we get "free thought" eventually driven to the conclusion that thought is not free at all, and rationalism surrendering to what is called "the scepticism of the instrument," namely the belief that the reason of man is incompetent to arrive at truth: which contains the contradiction of making a statement which it thinks ought to be accepted while denying

AUTHORITY

that there is any basis for such acceptance. The Catholic position does not make the Scripture the sole authority, neither does it isolate Christ, on the one hand, from all that went before Him, nor, on the other, from the unseen Father, and least of all from that human judgment to which He Himself appealed. It does not isolate the authority of the Church into a position which only makes it arbitrary; and least of all does it make the mere acceptance of all these consentient authorities equivalent to faith. There must be a subjective realization of objective truth brought home to the mind by converging and confirmatory authority. It also evades the popular misunderstanding of the Roman Catholic position, for which, however, Roman Catholic teachers are largely responsible, that Christianity consists simply in believing what the Church teaches. The true position is that the Church speaks with a solemn appeal to men, calling to witness the authority of reason and Scripture, prophetic promises and historic fulfilment, together with the experience of ten thousand saints, that these things are so; and bidding men seek the gift of faith and the grace of the Holy Spirit, which will make them real and powerful in mind, heart and life. This is the real authority of the Church, and every earnest soul must accept it and welcome it.

It might be questioned whether the notion of infallibility had not corrupted the very idea of authority, and by overweighting it caused its fall and rejection, especially in the form of papal infallibility. But it can be argued that the doctrine of papal infallibility is only a summing up of the infallibility of the Church; it only claims to operate within the area of faith and morals; it does not mean that any definitive statement is so made that it could not be better made and needs no

AUTHORITY

further explanation. It only means that the Church claims to carry on that line of revelation which, because it never contradicts itself, can be absolutely trusted. In the same way the Roman Catholic doctrine of the Scriptures need not involve what is called literal inspiration; it does not mean that we can look to the Scriptures for scientific declarations or necessarily for literal history; but the inerrancy of Scripture only means that by its general direction it will not lead men into error, especially if they will accept its interpretation as worked out by many minds all down the ages, which have not only thought freely about these subjects, but have thought together, and have also experienced their reality. To accept the Church's interpretation of the Scriptures is nothing more than to accept a wider, more patient, and all-inclusive view: the interpretation that sums up all things in Christ.

There still, however, remains the difficulty of what is to be done when a person finds his own reason, conscience or religious experience contrary to the teaching of the Church. Now, fortunately the teaching of the Roman Church is perfectly clear on this issue; it says he must follow his conscience and his religious experience. Although it might be argued that his conscience needed educating and his religious experience had been corrupted, until he has more light he can do no other, and although he ought to consider the danger of setting up his own authority against a greater authority, yet if he is sincere, his sincerity enables him to be counted as belonging to the soul of the Church.

There is still, however, the further question of what can be made of the authority of the Church when, as we have admitted, the Church's unity has been broken. There it has to be pointed out that it is on this question of authority that the Church

AUTHORITY

has been broken, and through authority being pressed beyond its legitimate sphere on one side, and the rejection of necessary authority on the other. But even in these conditions considerable authority remains. There is the agreement which still binds into one all Christian bodies, and with which they challenge and confront the world, namely the message that personal and social salvation are to be found only in obeying Christ. Then there is the agreement of the Catholic Churches concerning the Creeds. This is an authority which ought to be respected as ancient, necessary and unable to be replaced; and we may reasonably hope for the day when the Creeds will be accepted by all who are called Christian; it is only a misunderstanding of their place and purpose which has brought about their rejection in Christendom. There are, finally, those doctrines which the Roman Church alone holds, and which, just because of the solemnity of the claim with which they are made, also demand from all Christians a great respect; for it would involve us in strange consequences to assume that this historic Church, with such a descent, with such a world-wide communion, and claiming that infallibility which Christ wished His Church to have, should fall into positive doctrinal error; and we may hope that further interpretation of what is meant by these disputed doctrines on one side, as well as a growing recognition of what is involved in their rejection on the other, combined with repudiation of all false extensions of the doctrine of authority, will eventually bring Christendom into the same faith, when it will surely not be difficult to bring all Christians into one communion.

The authority of the Church is therefore directive, not coercive, and even where infallible, it must be confirmed by experience.

VII

THE SACRAMENTAL SYSTEM

THE Catholic type of Christianity is distinguished from the Protestant, among other characteristics, not only by the difference in the number of sacraments it recognizes and the importance it attaches to them, but by its elevation of the Sacramental System into the ordinary means of grace; which creates a different psychology and probably involves a different philosophy of religion. While Protestantism generally recognizes only two sacraments, Catholicism recognizes seven. In addition, Protestantism regards its sacraments only as signs and symbols, inclines to relegate them to a very subordinate place, and even shows a tendency towards abandoning them altogether. In Catholicism, sacramentalism dominates both public worship and devotional practice; in addition to the seven sacraments it employs a large number of other rites which are called sacramentals; and in general it always leans towards some form of physical or material expression of faith or worship.

It will be well to examine first of all the Protestant objection to sacramentalism. It used to object to seven sacraments because it believed Christ instituted only two; but this is no longer an acute issue, for it is merely a question of what act of Christ constitutes an institution, or whether the word " sacrament " should be employed to describe certain rites. Moreover, advanced Protestantism is now inclined to doubt whether Christ instituted even the rites of Baptism or the

THE SACRAMENTAL SYSTEM

Eucharist; for radical criticism has put forward the theory that sacraments are due to a later infiltration of paganism into the Christian religion. This hypothesis must be given further examination, but that can best be done when we come to discuss the Eucharist.

It is obvious that the root of the Protestant objection is founded upon its belief in the pure spirituality of the Christian religion, and therefore in the work of grace being necessarily due to immediate action upon the personality. It is held that material things cannot possibly convey spiritual grace : grace operates in the psychical not in the physical realm. It is this theory, rather than facts discoverable by criticism of the Scriptures or by tracing the Church's sacraments to the pagan mysteries, which is really responsible for the attitude of Protestantism, and it is on this point therefore that the discussion can most profitably fasten. The objection to the idea that spiritual grace can ever be conveyed by material means seems to rest finally upon the assumption that the two realms of matter and spirit are so separate that interaction between them is impossible. But this can hardly be a consciously held philosophy in these days, for it contradicts the general assumptions of common sense, is found impossible to carry out in actual practice, and is now scientifically disproved by the researches of modern psychology. Neither is it necessary to suspect the survival of the Manichæan heresy that matter is in itself evil, for it would involve the complete rejection of Christianity to hold that God did not create matter equally with spirit, and in particular the doctrine of the Incarnation. There may be a tendency to despise the material and physical unduly, but the fount of the Protestant objection to sacraments

THE SACRAMENTAL SYSTEM

seems to be a feeling that, for the highest needs of the spirit, action must be unmediated. It would be generally admitted that we are dependent in some degree upon our physical frame for our thoughts, our ideas, and our emotions, and on material things for our present existence, while we are almost entirely dependent upon them for conveying our thoughts, feelings, and intentions to our fellows. And it would be generally allowed that the spirit of man derives indirectly some spiritual benefit from physical movement, eating and drinking, actual contact with his fellows; and that the things he sees in nature rouse in him certain high emotions; while human art such as sculpture, painting or music can convey something richer and profounder in meaning, and more moving and mystical than anything conveyed through the printed page or the spoken word. So far the modern Protestant can be brought to agree with the Catholic, and it is now possible to assume acceptance of a fundamentally sacramentalist philosophy, namely, that the spiritual can be communicated through the material. The point at issue between Catholicism and Protestantism is no longer the acceptance of a sacramentalist philosophy; for common sense is bound to hold to that philosophy, rather than to an absolute idealism, an absolute materialism, or a realism which, while admitting the existence of both matter and spirit, denies all possibility of interaction. Indeed, the sacramental philosophy is now being widely accepted by thoughtful Protestants, and yet this position is often used only to object to special sacraments, in that it regards all things as sacramental, and not able to be made more so by any selective process or consecrative rite. Protestantism is now willing to adopt sacramentals in its worship: in the use

THE SACRAMENTAL SYSTEM

of architectural and artistic suggestion and symbolism; and can hardly object to these, when it has already admitted music, perhaps the most emotionally dangerous of all aids to worship. It is therefore willing to reconsider sacraments also on the level of sacramentals, that is as symbols of grace and as aids to faith; where it still remains unconvinced, on the defensive, and in protest, is when Catholicism makes any sacrament necessary to salvation, or teaches that it actually conveys grace. Protestantism feels that salvation must not depend upon anything accidental or arbitrary; grace can only be made accessible and effectual by purely spiritual means and methods; and saving grace can act only through immediate contact between the soul and God, the soul's response being purely an act of faith. In this conviction it would support itself by the principles and claims of mysticism.

It is at this point interesting to consider the fact that Catholicism, which has made so much of external sacraments, has also certainly made most of mystical development, so that it looks as if it is not only by keeping the two together that in Catholicism the mystical life has been saved from many of the errors and perversions into which elsewhere it is inclined to fall, but since the use of sacraments evidently encourages mystical development, the sacraments must be themselves capable of a mystical interpretation; which, as a matter of fact, is precisely what Catholicism actually believes.

Catholicism does not actually hold that any sacraments whatsoever are absolutely necessary to the salvation of any individual soul; they are only generally necessary: that is, to mankind as a whole, to the salvation of the whole man, and because of man's present natural conditions. Under com-

THE SACRAMENTAL SYSTEM

pletely supernatural conditions sacraments are entirely unnecessary. There is a mystical contact between God and the soul which, when it reaches its supreme height, dispenses not only with words, images, thoughts, and feelings, but in some degree temporarily suspends, as well as passes beyond bodily functions. But while such mystical development is the end of our salvation, in the present condition it is reached with difficulty, is always imperfect and intermittent, and therefore sacraments are needed. The Catholic theory only necessitates that the sacraments are *aids* to faith, and *means* of grace; certainly not that faith is unnecessary where they are employed, or that grace knows no other means. The actual issue therefore between a non-sacramental Protestantism and a sacramental Catholicism is largely due to an almost complete misunderstanding of what Catholic teaching about the sacraments actually is, and at the last comes down to a question of what is best for everybody on the whole, having in consideration the physical and psychological constitution of man. The mistake of Protestantism is, in the first instance, a fault of tactics in rejecting everything that has proved to be open to abuse instead of correcting the abuse by true teaching; secondly, in making individual experience a sufficient standard for all mankind; and thirdly, in selecting from that individual experience a certain spiritual height, once it is attained, and then failing to recognize what means were necessary to its attainment, and, since it is never completely attained in this life, the necessity for continuing these means even when such pure heights of spiritual experience have actually been reached.

It is at this point that the possibility of reconciling Catholic teaching with Protestant demand comes into view; for Catholics must admit that the sacra-

THE SACRAMENTAL SYSTEM

mental system is particularly liable to misunderstanding and abuse, it can rapidly descend into magical superstition, and the popular understanding, and a good deal of the common teaching about the sacraments, have indisputably ministered to a condition of things against which every protest ought to be raised. But, on the other hand, Protestants must recognise that this possibility of abuse follows everything good in this world, and the highest most of all, but is not to be remedied by the abandonment of what is in itself good. And especially do Protestants need to beware against the spiritual pride which always threatens those who profess that they do not need the help, which they are willing to admit others might need. It must therefore be noted that while in Catholicism the sacraments are *generally* necessary to salvation, faith is *always* necessary; sometimes to complete, as in the case of Baptism, sometimes to precede, as in the case of the Eucharist, but at some point or other always to co-operate. The sacraments are useless without faith; whereas faith can unite to Christ without the sacraments. But where faith is informed, where it knows its own imperfection and weakness, where it is concerned for the faith of others, it will welcome and crave and demand the sacraments. God can always dispense with His sacraments, but man must never try to do so. While Catholicism holds that the sacraments cause grace, this is not because they convey it naturally or magically, but by the action of God who has chosen this means. How actually the sacraments cause grace is even an open question in Catholic theology, some holding that they cause grace itself, or some only a title or disposition to grace; a distinction which becomes very minute, for a title to grace is itself an act of God's grace, and a disposition to grace is already an effect of grace.

THE SACRAMENTAL SYSTEM

It must therefore be remembered, though sometimes in Catholicism it seems to have been forgotten, that the sacraments must remain ineffectual without teaching: for instance, to baptize masses of heathen children, and then leave them to grow up without any instruction would negative the action of the sacrament. To give the sacrament of the Eucharist to those who had no knowledge whatsoever of what they were receiving would be not only useless, but sacrilegious, that is, it would be breaking the law of the sacrament. We shall probably be able to see further into the operation of sacramental law if we now turn to consider the actual working of three of the seven sacraments, namely: Penance, Holy Orders, and Baptism; leaving the Eucharist for separate treatment later, and taking these three sacraments in this order, because it is the order in which they can perhaps be the more easily comprehended.

The sacrament of *Penance* depends more than any other sacrament, save marriage, which is practically self-administered, upon the disposition of the recipient. No absolution is of any avail unless the confession has been integral and there is true contrition. Indeed, it is held that wherever perfect contrition is present it brings with it perfect absolution. Perfect contrition, however, must be difficult to attain, and may be safely reckoned to be very rare. What the sacrament of Penance does is to give us grace to make up for our falling short of perfect contrition; and because of the merit attaching to the actual making of a confession, because of the sincere desire for forgiveness thus expressed, and through the authoritative word of the priest whom the Church has appointed for this purpose, the absolving declaration does bring actual release, not only from the burden, but from the guilt of sin. The grace of absolution may be discerned in action

THE SACRAMENTAL SYSTEM

because it moves the soul to a deeper penitence, and because the word of authority releases the mind from any longer carrying the burden of its sin. The psychological effects of confession are now generally admitted, and for the quietening of conscience and the relief of the mind they are often absolutely necessary for the final setting free of a soul; and from these psychological effects we can well understand why God has chosen these means of grace which are best suited to our nature. Therefore, the difficulties felt about a sacrament seem to vanish at this point, where co-operation is seen to be so necessary, and the actual effects can be discerned. When the Catholic system demands that confession is obligatory, it does so only for the sake of the whole body of the Church; and it would not only be highly temerarious, but spiritually suspicious for any individual to contract out of this system because he felt it to be unnecessary for him. But, on the other hand, not only is absolution dependent upon some degree of real penitence and the exercise of all possible sincerity, but there is no necessity to argue that its effects upon all shall be seen to be equally salutary. Not only can a confession be sacrilegious, but the sacrament can be wrongly used so that it weakens or even depraves character. There is no safeguard in this world which will prevent human nature from crossing the divine purpose or hindering the divine intention. Every means must be taken to prevent this by diligent instruction both inside and outside the confessional. This sacrament should not be abandoned because it may sometimes have been abused by wicked confessors, or its effects weakened by penitents of little understanding; for these things no more disprove its general value or provide an argument for dispensing with its necessity, than the frightful abuses and sometimes

THE SACRAMENTAL SYSTEM

weakening effects of marriage are an argument against its necessity for the continuance of the human race or its value for the development of character.

Difficulties attending the Sacramental System are apparently felt somewhat more acutely in regard to the sacrament of *Holy Orders*; which in particular is held to bestow upon a man a character which makes him the representative of Christ at the Eucharist and gives to him power to absolve sins. Merely on lines of representation it would be easy to gain an understanding that ordination is simply a commission conveyed by those who represent the whole Church, and therefore carries with it the authority and should receive the recognition of the whole Church. But it is held to be a sacrament, and not merely an official act. What, then, is this sacrament supposed to convey? It is something more than the *right* to represent the Church in the offering of the Eucharist or in the pronouncing of absolution. It is held to convey a grace which enables the priest to discharge those duties. There can be no idea that the grace then bestowed is invincible; that notion is explicitly condemned by Catholicism as contrary to the Christian faith and divine revelation. What we can really look for then is a special divine incentive to a holy life. It is easy to understand that the very nature of the duties which the priest is called upon to perform continually confronts him with the demand that his life and his thought shall conform to what he is constantly called upon to do; and these are, of course, the means that God actually uses to make grace efficacious. But the outward act of ordination is a sign given by God, both to the person ordained and to the whole Church, that sufficient grace shall always be given. Whether it is used or not depends first upon the person ordained, and secondly upon the general spiritual state of the Church. What is the measure of the grace thus given, and whether it does actually make any difference, ought to be capable of an empirical test; and it is to such a test that Protestants who do not believe in the grace of Orders sometimes confidently appeal. They point out how men have sprung up outside the ecclesiastical system, have been rejected by the authorities, or sometimes actually ejected from the Church, who, by their life and their spiritual power, have manifested that they possess a grace either independent of Orders or actually superior to anything visible within the recognized order. As a matter of fact, we are here inviting a comparison which it is exceedingly difficult to bring to an actual test. It would not only have to be confined to areas where all other possible causes were equally active, but it would have to be spread over long periods of time in order to see the working out of its effect. No Catholic theory demands a denial that God can and does raise up prophets and preachers outside the ecclesiastical system; it does not even deny that any individual may actually possess the full priestly powers which are given in ordination. Nevertheless, the theory of the sacramental character of Holy Orders does involve that there shall be a certain discernible character within the sacerdotal order, which is not so generally discernible outside. And, on the whole, this can be fairly well established, despite dreadful defects and horrible inconsistencies, which it will be admitted have sometimes disgraced the Catholic clergy. On the other hand, they have often reached a stage of sanctity which no one outside approaches or attempts; and although they may often not possess those gifts which have enabled individuals outside

THE SACRAMENTAL SYSTEM

the order to do signal work for God, they have, however, established a great reputation for spiritual power and influence, and there is more often found among them the grace of humility and sanctified common sense. It is obvious that the Church of God cannot depend solely upon prophetic preachers or men of unusual spiritual power; often when such arise they do not build up the Church or leave a permanent spiritual effect. There is, no doubt, great need for better teaching concerning the priesthood, and greater readiness to recognize the call of God which has come to great souls and to make room for them within the system, as well as to expect and recognize that they will often spring up outside it, and for various reasons remain outside it. On the other hand, those who are truly called of God should be all the more willing to recognize the need of the Church's commission, and if they are men of real spirituality, they will be the first to seek for any means of grace open to them, and will not rely too much on their natural gifts or their own efforts in attempting to do Christ's work in the world. We may conclude that the sacrament of Holy Orders does convey the grace which is necessary to equip the ordinary man for the sacred ministry and to make him a worthy pastor for the shepherding of the one flock.

It is, however, when we come to the sacrament of *Baptism* that the difficulties of the Sacramental System are most acutely felt, particularly when Baptism normally takes place in infancy; for then the co-operation of faith is postponed, and we have to rely upon the faith of the Church which receives the child; and until the child itself comes to faith it is difficult to see what grace can be conveyed by this sacrament, especially when Catholicism claims that what is received in Baptism is nothing less

THE SACRAMENTAL SYSTEM

than regeneration. The objection to "baptismal regeneration" is, however, generally due to a misunderstanding of what is meant by regeneration. It is not conversion, still less is it the gift of final salvation; it is simply the reinstatement of the soul to the status it lost through original sin, namely, the restoration to the soul of the capacity for being lifted to a supernatural life. Before this is further explained it would be well for it to be recognized that, in rejecting this as the meaning of Baptism, Protestantism obviously does not know what to make of the rite. When it is deliberately taught that Baptism is only a sign of grace otherwise conveyed, then obviously it can be omitted without serious loss; and despite the desire to find some meaning for the rite, and to retain an ancient and universal practice of the Church, it tends to get omitted. And if it is only a sign of that universal grace which it must be believed God offers to all men who are born into this world, the omission of the sign can make no difference whatsoever. If, again, it is only a sign of a sufficient faith already reached, as it is when only administered to an adult on profession of faith, then again it becomes essentially unnecessary, and is only retained in obedience to what is believed to be a command of our Lord, for which, however, there can be given no rational explanation. Where what is called Believers' Baptism is practised, it shows every sign of eventually dying out altogether. The Catholic, on the contrary, will try to overcome every possible difficulty, and eliminate every point of doubt, in order to secure that a child shall be properly baptized before it dies. It will obviously not be sufficient to maintain the Catholic faith concerning Baptism simply because it makes the rite necessary and is therefore the best means of securing that the rite

THE SACRAMENTAL SYSTEM

shall be observed and continued for all time; we must seek a deeper necessity than that.

What, then, does Catholicism hold that there is bestowed in Baptism? It holds that grace is bestowed to enable the child to be called a child of God, and to attain the full Christian salvation. But while effective for that, it is neither coercive nor exclusive. It is not exclusive of other means of grace. God gives to all men grace enough, if they use their reason, to believe in His existence. Moreover, it is Catholic teaching that if anyone desires what Baptism gives he actually receives the Baptism of desire; and this, even though he may have conscientious objection to being baptized at all, believing it to be a meaningless rite or a misunderstanding of our Lord's words, as a sincere Quaker might do; even when he knows nothing about the rite of Baptism at all, or is living in entire ignorance of Christianity, yet if, by some hidden means, he comes to desire what it gives he will receive it. The future condition of the heathen demands a discussion that must be given a fuller place later on; but the omission of Baptism obviously raises no other difficulty than that of souls born in heathendom. Baptism conveys nothing more immediately than the removal of the penalty attaching to Original Sin. The meaning of Original Sin has been discussed previously; here it must suffice to say that by it man is reduced to a merely natural level, and the way to a supernatural life of union with God is barred to him until he repents. Now Baptism conveys a grace which urges the soul to repentance. Baptism is "*unto* remission of sins"; that is, it has this as its purpose; and therefore the removal of the preliminary hindrance is what Baptism actually effects. It is obvious why this can be given to a child, for there must always be such grace bestowed before repentance is possible. But if such grace is a necessary preliminary, and it can be bestowed upon an infant, the question naturally arises, why God does not bestow this on every child at its birth, and not make it dependent upon Baptism. But here there comes in the fact that the sacrament of Baptism, like all the other sacraments, is the act of the Church. The re-investment of human souls with the capacity for union with God is a social and corporate matter; for just as the soul of man cannot grow to consciousness as an isolated individual, neither can it be brought into conscious communion with God, apart from the co-operation of such already conscious of God. Therefore it is only by being incorporated into the communion of the Church that the salvation of any individual soul can be perfected. It is by the faith, and into the faith, of the Church that the baptized child is received, and it is in answer therefore to the prayers of the Church that the child is given that grace which makes possible its attainment of supernatural life. All we need say about infants dying unbaptized is that supernatural salvation is not possible to them; but all that is possible to natural humanity is not only open, but, if they have never lived to commit conscious sin, is assured to them; and this involves not only natural happiness, but a natural knowledge of God in which they are perfectly happy. To the baptized there is given grace which makes it possible to attain to union with God. This is something which does more than restore man to his condition before the Fall. Then, we may conceive, communion with God was possible to man; but now, more than that is possible, namely, union with God, an entirely supernatural thing; for we are baptized *into* the name of the Father, and of the Son, and of the Holy Ghost; that is, potentially admitted into a share of the Divine nature. Simply

THE SACRAMENTAL SYSTEM

not to have this is no deprivation, for it is no part of man's national endowment or even capacity. Whatever advantage this gift brings, it also brings with it a further responsibility; for if this grace is not used, then the soul comes under condemnation. Some might still want to raise the question, What would happen if the Church simply prayed that the child might receive God's grace, but did not use water? Now it is obvious that the water itself does not cleanse the child from original sin; it is the sign, however, that when water is used God does bestow that gift. If any people refused to use water, then by that act they would profess themselves willing to dispense with God's sign that such grace was given, and by their pride they would not only be wronging the child, but proclaiming themselves to be children of disobedience. If anyone demands an empirical test that Baptism makes any real difference he must abide by the conditions which such a test involves. It cannot be decided by any crude method such as the difference between two persons, one of whom has been baptized and the other has not. It would not even be fair to take the general character, say, of Quakers, and the general character of Catholics; for, after all, the Quakers are living inside a baptized community. It would not be sufficient to disprove the efficacy of Baptism to point out that there were worse scoundrels within Christendom than could be found in heathendom; or that men of great uprightness, spiritual vision, or sanctity could be found in heathendom. All that can be demanded as satisfying the test is that the saints of Christendom should be more advanced, numerous and continuous. And this test could be claimed to stand not only between Christendom and heathendom, but between Catholicism, which baptizes, and any form of Christianity which does not. With the practice of Baptism

THE SACRAMENTAL SYSTEM

demoniac influences seem to disappear, and there is no assurance that if Baptism is given up they will not return—indeed, there is accumulating evidence to the contrary. For the Church to offer Baptism, and the parents to seek it for a child, is the highest possible endowment with which a soul can be started on its earthly career, for there is thereby claimed for it the grace which, if rightly used, will bring it into union with God. Wilfully to neglect Baptism is to do that soul a grievous wrong, and to dispense with it on some anti-sacramental conviction is to dispense with the divine assurance while professing faith in the divine intention, a curiously irreligious attitude. Conscientiously to postpone Baptism until the child can choose for itself is nevertheless to overlook the necessity for God's prevenient grace on which all salvation depends.

The Sacramental System is an interweaving of human effort to convey spiritual gifts to men, and the divine assurance that it is being done according to the divine desire; and there is every reason to believe that, where it is rightly administered and its principles understood, it maintains the most constant witness to the realities of the spiritual life, it is the greatest general incentive to a holy life, and it makes for the sanctification of the whole physical and material order; sacraments and sacramentals being anticipations of the redemption of all things and their true relation to the spiritual order.

VIII

THE EUCHARIST

CATHOLIC doctrine maintains that in the Holy Eucharist the Body and Blood of Christ are present on the altar, because the bread and the wine there set apart are transformed into the Body and Blood of Christ by the act of consecration; these are then able to be offered as a sacrifice, in the same way as Christ offered Himself on Calvary, for the sins of the world; and, being received, they effect the union of the soul with Christ crucified, to which all the benefits of His Passion are thereby immediately imparted. From this doctrine there naturally follows the immense importance given to the Eucharist: it is made the chief and central act of worship; communion becomes the highest means of grace; and the consecrated elements objects of devout adoration. But this interpretation of the Eucharist has now long been challenged by Protestants as due to an unnatural and childish literalism in the interpretation of Christ's words at the institution of the Sacrament; as involving a stupendous and incredible miracle; as infringing the perfect sacrifice of Christ offered once for all upon the cross; and as leading to an idolatrous and degrading worship of mere bread and wine. It is to this complete misunderstanding of Christ's words and the perversion of His intention that there are to be traced the magical notions, the superstitious accretions, and the reliance upon attendance at a rite for securing the favour of God, and upon mere physical acts as guaranteeing

THE EUCHARIST

the operation of grace, which generally accompany popular Catholicism. No candid and well-informed Catholic would deny that there are popular misunderstandings and very superficial understanding of what the Eucharist involves; many superstitions and abuses have gathered round the Mass, and mechanical notions of its efficacy have prevailed. These things Protestants believe to be natural and inseparable consequences of a perverted theory which, in the language common to ruder times, has been described as a blasphemous fable and a dangerous deceit; it is this which has given false powers to a corrupt priesthood and is responsible for the moral deterioration of Catholic populations.

Before attempting to set forth what the true Catholic doctrine is, to prove that it is true to Scripture and not responsible for whatever misunderstanding, abuses or corruptions have become connected with it, it would be convenient to enquire what then is the Protestant understanding of Christ's intention in arranging for a celebration of the Passover with His disciples, and thereat initiating a new rite, and what therefore is the right observance of the Lord's Supper and the true doctrine of what has come to be called the Eucharist. In endeavouring to answer that question we are, however, faced with the awkward fact that there are various interpretations within Protestantism. These have been tabulated by Catholic apologists as reaching an immense number, but we need only concern ourselves with the main varieties. It must be noted at the outset, however, that these arrange themselves in a descending order, the lower interpretation promising greater simplicity of observance and an easier understanding of its meaning, yet as the mystery of the words of institution is progressively diminished, resulting ultimately in the twisting of

THE EUCHARIST

the intention of Christ's words to the exact opposite of what was actually said, so that the meaning becomes almost " this is *not* my Body ; this is *not* my Blood " ; the celebration of the Eucharist is reduced from an ornate and dignified ceremony to an attenuated and sometimes slovenly rite, with a tendency to more infrequent celebrations, which thereby testifies to the prevalence of a lower estimate of its value as a means of grace.

Perhaps the highest form of interpretation next to that maintained by Catholic doctrine is that known as Consubstantiation, the theory advocated by Luther, namely :, that the Body and Blood of Christ are really and truly present, but alongside the bread and wine which remain themselves unchanged. There seem to be echoes of this theory discernible in the words of the Consecration Prayer in the Book of Common Prayer (" Grant that we receiving these Thy creatures of bread and wine . . . may be partakers of His most blessed Body and Blood ") ; in the theory put forward by some Anglican theologians that the Real Presence is only conditionally attached to the sacred species, since they may be withdrawn if they are used for any unauthorised purpose ; as well as in the generally hesitant attitude towards extra-liturgical worship and devotions in connection with the Reserved Sacrament. It should be noted, however, that this attitude is often maintained along with an emphatic belief in the Real Presence ; all that is denied is that any change takes place in the bread and wine. Where the influence of Calvin has extended and remains, there may be a belief in some special presence of Christ at the Lord's Supper, but this is not regarded as in any way attached to the bread and wine, but is rather granted in obedience to the devout observance of the rite, which is a setting

THE EUCHARIST

forth of Christ's death under the symbols of broken bread and outpoured wine, in which those who participate by faith receive a special grace, namely the application to their souls of the benefits of Christ's redeeming Passion. We have here a purely spiritual interpretation of Christ's presence concomitant with the eating and drinking of bread and wine, imparting grace, however, only to the person who has the faith to discern Christ and spiritually to receive Him. This Calvinistic theory, although capable of maintaining a high value for the Sacrament as a means of grace, always tends to decline into the still lower valuation of the Zwinglian interpretation, which makes the observance of the Lord's Supper a merely memorial rite, with what benefit there comes from an act of obedience, devotion being quickened by the mnemonic of the rite, nothing, however, being derived from the observance save that possible to the mental associations and the spiritual condition which the observant already brings to it.

Under these three theories the rite is still observed, though naturally with declining frequency, attraction, or even intelligibility; for under none of them does communion with Christ sought through such means seem to disclose anything more than an arbitrary, accidental, or psychological necessity, which individuals, who are so constituted that they are only confused by an external rite or the use of material symbols, may abandon without serious loss, finding, as they do, direct spiritual communion a simpler and more profitable way. But the Quaker theory takes the logical conclusion and abandons the rite altogether; though not simply following the natural tendency, but on the conscientious ground of a conviction that Christ never intended to institute a rite at all; Christ's intention at the

THE EUCHARIST

Last Supper being nothing more than to inculcate the practice of thinking of Him whenever we eat or drink, thus making every meal a sacrament. It should be noted in all these theories that they each insist upon something that the Catholic theory also holds, namely: the Real Presence, the representation of Christ's death, the rite being a memorial feast, and even the Quaker interpretation that all meals are by this sacrament elevated and sanctified. But falling short of the Catholic theory they fail to guarantee the Real Presence from possible withdrawal even when the consecrated elements remain; they do not provide an adequate spiritual necessity for the observance of the rite; they evacuate Christ's words of the depth and the rite of the mystery, which in the great solemnity of the occasion obviously attach to them; or they attempt to extend the area of sacramental significance while at the same time weakening the centre from which alone it is derived.

We need not examine these theories one by one to show how, in the endeavour to confine themselves to what the Scriptures alone sanction, they fail to embody as much as the Scriptures demand; for Protestant scholarship has now moved to a much further extreme, and radical criticism has put forward the position that Christ never instituted a rite at all, the account in the Gospels being an interpolation introduced in order to justify the sacramental observance which had developed, but which had been derived, neither from the teaching nor the intention of Christ, but as a matter of fact, from the pagan mysteries. St. Paul is regarded as the real originator of the Eucharist in the Christian Church, and the regulations he laid down for the Corinthian Church are taken to be not only the earliest witness of the observance of the Sacrament, but disclose the founder of the observance. This

THE EUCHARIST

theory demands careful examination, but it may be noted at the outset, that two conclusions may be drawn from its acceptance. It might be concluded that St. Paul, although the actual originator of the observance, was nevertheless acting under a true revelation which has proved of great spiritual value to the development of the Church and the continuance of the devout life; but, on the other hand, it might be concluded that St. Paul was responsible for the unfortunate introduction of sacraments into the Christian system, for sacraments have been designated as the "disease of Christianity." This extreme position nevertheless claims support from the genuine teaching and general spiritual outlook of Jesus, to whose ascertainable mind any form of sacramentalism is declared to be utterly alien. Others, less concerned to maintain Christ's freedom from these contaminating ideas, trace their germ at any rate to Him, and, therefore, look upon Christianity as a form of religion too corrupted at its fount to be of any further value to the emancipated mind and the purely spiritual idealism of modern man.

We must refer back to our general discussion concerning the basis of the Sacramental System, and look forward to a subsequent discussion on Christ's attitude towards ritual, as a refutation of the extreme opposition to sacramentalism. But we must give some further consideration at this point to the more generous estimate of sacramentalism which would nevertheless refuse to admit that the Eucharist was founded by Christ. The critical basis for this position is founded, first of all, upon the fact that St. Paul declares that he had "received of the Lord" the instructions which he commands the Corinthians to put into operation. But there is no indication that by these words St. Paul meant that his instructions had been received of the Lord immediately by means of a revelation; moreover, even if it were so, it was a revelation not simply of what the Corinthian Church ought to do, but of the fact that Jesus instituted such a rite " in the night in which He was betrayed." It is unlikely that any such revelation would have been accepted by the Church if it had not been already held as a tradition and testified to by the Apostles who had actually been present at the Last Supper. But it is supposed that some basis is given for the dependence of this tradition on later revelation in that St. Luke gives a much simpler account of what actually happened, if what is alleged to be the true text is followed. His narrative of the Last Supper opens with a reference to Christ receiving a cup at a meal, which was either the Passover or some preliminary anticipation of it, and simply telling the disciples to drink it amongst themselves, proclaiming that He would not drink of it until the Kingdom came. In the ordinary text there then follows a description of the institution of the Eucharist, which is almost word for word that given in the First Epistle to the Corinthians. From its close similarity it looks as if this passage might be a later interpolation from Corinthians, especially as it introduces the confusion of a reference to two cups. There is, however, no textual testimony for the entire omission of this passage, though a small family of manuscripts which embody what is called the Western Text do omit the words " which is given for you . . . which is poured out for you"; this therefore says nothing about the exhortation to continue the rite in Christ's memory, and does not refer to any cup other than that already mentioned, thus omitting any identification of the cup with the New Covenant in Christ's Blood. But even if this omission of the Western text should represent the

THE EUCHARIST

original, a highly disputable point, it would then diminish the likeness to the Corinthian Epistle, and any suspicion that it was an interpolation therefrom; while the sacramental witness would not be entirely eliminated, for the reduced Lucan text still contains the declaration " this is my Body." Moreover, both St. Matthew and St. Mark contain an explicit account of Christ's act in taking bread and a cup, and in saying over them " this is my body . . . this is my blood of the covenant, which is shed for many "; so that, even if St. Matthew merely copied from St. Mark, we have a fully sacramental description of the Last Supper in our earliest Gospel, to which the critics generally give very high authority, and there is no textual evidence whatever for its omission. Radical critics are, however, always prepared to go behind the text, and, they conjecture that Christ celebrated the Passover, or something like it, perhaps bidding His friends farewell over the final cup in such a way as to make it very solemn and memorable. The repetition of this rite was due to no command or intention of Christ; but it is easy to imagine that when afterwards the Apostles met for a common meal, the blessing and sharing of the bread, and the solemn partaking of a cup of fellowship, brought the last meal with Christ and His presence so vividly before them, that this became a regular observance, and was gradually filled out with ideas derived from the pagan mysteries. It need hardly be pointed out these are mere conjectures, they can never be anything else, and they are not only unprovable, but are in themselves highly unlikely. Their only support is the admitted likeness between the developed observance of the Eucharist and elements in some of the mysteries, which, indeed, so struck some of the Fathers that they referred them to diabolic imitation. The degree of dependence of

THE EUCHARIST

Christianity upon the pagan mysteries is too complicated a subject to be investigated in any fullness here, but it may be safely said, in the first place, that we know very little for certain about the "mysteries"; secondly, that the resemblance between them and the Christian Sacraments is slight, sporadic, and in some cases the dependence is likely to be in the other direction; thirdly, from what we know of the Jewish attitude in general, and St. Paul's in particular, to pagan ideas and worship, it is unthinkable that anything should have been directly adopted from such sources. There is another explanation which fits in with what is maintained in a previous discussion under Comparative Religion: that there has been in all religions some groping after a sacramentalism, of which the Christian Eucharist is its spiritual realization and perfect fulfilment. The origin of the Eucharist is in some way or other certainly connected with the Passover, and is therefore derivable more naturally from the Jewish type of "mysteries," namely, the sacrifices of the Levitical system, of which, as a matter of fact, the words of the Institution are directly reminiscent.

It is instructive, however, to notice that the extreme views which would deny the institution of the Eucharist to Christ, are thereby all the more free to interpret the meaning of St. Paul's reference to the observance; and many advanced scholars have been driven to conclude from them that St. Paul was a high sacramentalist, and that his condemnation of those who did not discern the Lord's Body and his declaration that those who ate and drank unworthily were guilty of the Body and Blood of Christ demand a theory equivalent to the doctrine of the Real Presence. Some advanced scholars also see in the sixth chapter of St. John not only an exposition of the

THE EUCHARIST

Sacrament, but a theory of it which approximates to the doctrine of Transubstantiation. The freest radical scholarship has therefore been compelled to read sacramentalism back to a very early stage in Christianity. It finds it already in the New Testament; and it would be pushing it only a step further back to refer it to the teaching of Christ, and to find it embodied in the institution of that ceremonial rite, which either followed after or anticipated the Passover, and if so, must have been intended by Christ to take its place as the sacrificial observance of His disciples and as a means of His being united with them in a new covenant. This seems a far more natural origin for the undoubtedly early observance of the Eucharist than any derivation from the pagan mysteries.

Although sacrificial language only gradually became more definite and sacramental theory developed only instinctively, there was no questioning of such interpretation until the teaching of Scotus Erigena, and the ensuing Berengarian controversy; this, however, stiffened into opposition under the protest of Wycliffe, broke out in violence at the Reformation, and ever since has contributed one of the chief elements in the Protestant resistance to Catholicism. But, as we have seen, Protestantism is now in considerable difficulty, not only about the interpretation, but even about the continuance of the Eucharistic rite. Radical criticism, while still refusing to ascribe the institution of the rite to Christ, which conservative Protestants, however, still maintain, demands the carrying back of the sacramental idea to an even earlier time, and so by a circuitous route advanced thought is making for a reconsideration of the sacramental notion. It is therefore not beside the point, and a hopeful method of approach, to consider the lines on which it is conceivable that Protestant-

THE EUCHARIST

ism may gradually return to the Catholic interpretation of the Sacrament. The modern emphasis upon the psychological effects of worship and the recognition of the value of symbols may tend to restore the sacramental rite as a necessity at least for any corporate sense of personal communion with Christ. But the modern mind can hardly rest content for long with mere psychology, or with the retention of a merely symbolic rite; it is all too reminiscent of kindergarten methods; it must seek a rational basis for a psychological necessity, and a theological explanation for the undying attraction which it is ever more widely admitted that the Mass exerts over devout and discerning minds. Some Protestant scholars have suggested that in the words " this is My body," " this " includes the whole rite, and " My body " refers to the Church; when the words simply mean that in the rite of a common meal the Church and Christ gather together at His table. But apart from the strain this puts upon these words, no such interpretation is possible in regard to the words " this is My blood "; and although the New Testament does use the words " the body of Christ" for the Church, that cannot be the meaning here, for we cannot be invited to eat the Church. Some Protestant thinkers have been attracted by the theory of impanation, as a sufficient explanation of Christ's words, namely: that just as by His incarnation Christ used His physical body to bring Himself into contact with men, so He now uses the bread and the wine to establish a still closer contact. This enables the bread and wine to be spoken of as His Body and His Blood, because it is for that He now uses them. But apart from the fact, which will carry very little weight with many Protestants, that this is the very heresy put forward by Berengarius, condemned by the Church and by him afterwards

THE EUCHARIST

retracted, such a theory is quite inadequate to the words " this is My body *which is given for you* ; this is My blood of the new covenant *which is shed for many*," for this identifies the Body and the Blood with the very body that suffered and the blood that was shed on Calvary. Some modern Protestant thinkers, however, dissatisfied with the strictly substitutionary and merely forensic doctrine of the Atonement, are seeking after some mystical identification with Christ, in which, at any rate, the Atonement needs to be consummated in order to take effect in the individual soul, and they are beginning to feel the attraction of the theory underlying the Mass, because in the Communion the believer can be sacramentally incorporated into Christ, and His Blood mystically applied to their hearts ; in short, being crucified with Christ is recognized to be both essential to any efficient theory of the Atonement, and it is discerned that this is actually the inner meaning of the Mass.

Further, the modern discoveries of the constitution of matter and of the possibility of the transmutation of the elements, while of course providing no explanation whatever of Transubstantiation, this being a change which is considered as taking place in a completely insensible realm, and being anyhow of an almost opposite character, nevertheless has removed from the modern mind the sheer inconceivability and, therefore, the incredibility of a substantial change in the elements being possible. It seems only necessary, as a further step, to gain a hearing for the real meaning of Transubstantiation. Even among those who believe that they hold the Catholic doctrine of the Eucharist it has been objected that Transubstantiation is a purely Roman Catholic doctrine because it only received its formal definition at the Council of Trent ; but the word had been used to describe the change that takes

THE EUCHARIST

place in the elements at consecration long before that time. Transubstantiation is, moreover, nothing but the proper Latin translation of the word that the Greek Church uses to describe the change, namely, *metousiosis*. When, further, it is grasped that in the scholastic terminology " substance " means the very opposite to what it means in modern English, and that Transubstantiation is a change that takes place in an entirely invisible, non-spatial and intangible realm, it can be understood that no material miracle is involved, for the change which takes place is not strictly in the natural order at all. The Tridentine doctrine is not even to be taken as necessarily involving the mediæval philosophy of substance and accidents, for the word " accidents " is expressly avoided in the definitions of Trent. Further, there is no actual definition of what is meant by the substance of the bread and wine ; all that is involved is that it is something which underlies the appearance that is subject to the change ; and all common sense is compelled to believe that there is such a thing, for a thing is not identical with its appearance. Moreover, it should be carefully noted, since it often seems to be overlooked in popular Roman Catholic exposition, that the substance of the bread and wine is not declared to be converted simply into the Body and Blood of Christ, but into the *substance* of the Body and Blood ; when all possibility of carnal misunderstanding is removed. When it is grasped, as Catholic theology has definitely laid down, that there is no movement of Christ's natural body in any movement of the sacramental species, that the ultimate reality of the Sacrament is therefore not in space at all, it begins to be seen that whether the doctrine of Transubstantiation be metaphysically true or not, it is the most spiritual interpretation of the Eucharist that has so far been conceived. If it has a fault at all, it is in the danger of over-refining, rather than of materializing the meaning of Christ's actual words. The devout Protestant communicant who desires communion with his Lord can easily be brought to believe that by the reception of the sacred species he is inviting Christ into his heart, who through this means offers to him that ultimate, objective, spiritual reality, which was the substance of His offering of Himself on the Cross. It is only a step further to believe that the sacred species are substantially identical with that very same Christ, who became incarnate, and who hung upon the Cross for us, and whose humanity is now glorified, so that at the Communion there is received the inner reality of Calvary and all that was expressed in the giving of His body and the shedding of His blood. Indeed, it does not seem difficult to see the possibility of one who accepts a high Calvinistic view of the Sacrament passing over by insensible stages, and yet with immense gain in the sense of reality and efficacy, to the full Catholic view. Further, the Sacrifice of the Mass is explicitly declared to be neither an addition to, nor a repetition of, Calvary, but the very same offering as that made on Calvary. Since Christ offered Himself by an eternal spirit, this can be continually represented in time as it was on Calvary; save that in the Mass it is now an unbloody sacrifice that is offered, for it is one with the eternal offering which Christ is now making for us in heaven; wherefore it is not so much that Christ comes down to us upon the Altar, but through the Sacrifice of the Altar we are brought into touch with the offering which Christ ever lives to make for us in the heavenly realm, and at the Mass we are actually partaking in the worship of the Lamb once slain and now standing upon the throne. At

THE EUCHARIST

this point all difficulty seems to disappear, the elevated Host and the uplifted Chalice being the representation of an eternal fact, and the consecrated species the union between earthly and heavenly realities.

Finally, when it is understood that worthy participation in this rite demands a sincere desire to be united with Christ in His redeeming Passion, to which He calls us by the display of His loving condescension and which He established this rite to show forth and effect, its supreme devotional value will be realised and its sanctifying power sought by all who aspire to be transformed into Christ's image. Where this is not understood the Mass loses its efficacy, and where this is evaded the rite is being sacrilegiously used. But in however careless, slovenly or sacrilegious a way the rite is performed, Christ is always truly present, and is always offering Himself for us and to us for the sake of the whole world. This is the objective reality which no unworthiness of celebrant or carelessness of communicant can affect. Although the Mass holds an objective reality which does not wait upon our faith, its subjective realization demands faith on our side; and although Christ is present and the fruits of His Passion are presented to us, without faith this will do us no more good than Calvary did to many who actually beheld it; like that it will work our condemnation if it does not win us nearer to the Crucified. There can, therefore, be no suspicion that the Mass is magical or the grace it conveys mechanical: everything still depends on faithful participation. But, in the Catholic theory, faith is brought into action at the right point; not as in some even high Protestant theories creating the Presence, or conditioning the reception of Christ's true Body and Blood; but creating a worthy reception, and conditioning the efficacy of the offered grace.

The use of the common necessities of our physical sustenance as a means of communion sets forth the wondrous humility of Christ, and the Mass carries with it the corollary doctrine that our common necessities are capable of being sanctified if they are manufactured in purity, offered in worship, and shared in common. In the setting apart of bread and wine for their sacred use matter is elevated to its highest level, and the consecrated Host is a promise, as it is an anticipation, of the redemption of all *things*. Therefore the Eucharist carries with it the supreme social sanction and command, as well as the deepest devotional demand and inspiration. Here then the craving of the soul for communion with Christ, and the provision of this institution meet in a wonderful way; the objective and the subjective, the individual and the social, the eternal and the temporal, the invisible and the visible are fused together. No wonder that to the experience of Catholics the Altar is the meeting-place of heaven and earth, the creative and the attracting centre of worship, the trysting-place between Christ and the soul; and we may well hope that the Mass will one day be discerned by all Christians to be the one thing that matters, the Catholic celebration the point at which unity will be found, and the doctrine of Transubstantiation the basis of a sacramental philosophy which illumines many mysteries, the sure foundation on which a truly corporate life can be built, the centre from which all our efforts at social reconstruction will be truly inspired.

IX

RITUAL

CATHOLIC worship is accustomed to employ a considerable quantity of ceremonial. It tends to express itself in outward acts, to move about from place to place, to make processions, to adopt varying postures in prayer, to use symbolic gestures, like the laying on of hands or the making of the sign of the cross; it employs material things like light, incense, water, salt, oil; it adopts a distinctive dress for worship, using different garments for different occasions. In the course of time ceremonial has naturally grown elaborate, has had to be regulated by authoritative prescription, and has become invested with mystical significance; it is often gorgeous and majestic, impressive even to those who do not understand its necessity or meaning, while to those who accept it and have long been accustomed to its use, it is laden with devotional association and is therefore profoundly moving.

This use of ceremony in worship has been one of the points at which Protestantism has revolted, while Puritanism has supported its intense dislike of ceremonial by a series of reasoned objections. Ceremonial is alleged to be a conception of the inwardness and simplicity of that religion which Christ came to establish; it is the reintroduction of elements which the most far-sighted of Israel's prophets had begun to condemn as detracting from true worship; much of it can be traced to heathen origins and is a condescension to pagan

RITUAL

practices; it ends by making external observances a substitute for spiritual worship, and embodies a childish and irreverent conception of what God demands in His service. The principle condemned is often stigmatized as formalism or ritualism. But there is no real reason why the use of outward forms, which in some degree is inevitable, should degenerate into formalism: that is, the employment of forms which are meaningless in themselves, whose inner significance is denied, forgotten or neglected, and with the conscious purpose of evading the demands of interior religion. For it is a significant and indisputable fact that it is in the very Church which has made most of external observance and has employed the greatest wealth of ceremonial that there has been the most careful, continuous and advanced cultivation of a mystical spirituality, so rare as to transcend even the possibility of being described in words, save as the merest symbols; while in that same communion whole movements have arisen and many individual experiments have been made to reduce personal life to the most rigorous simplicity, and even to stark and almost inhuman austerity. So that even if the employment of outward ceremony has too often been accompanied by a careless life, and the form has been made a substitute for the inward offering, this must not be regarded as a natural and inevitable consequence. There is no high and beautiful thing that man is not capable of perverting; he is continually attempting to evade spiritual demands, but there is no evidence that this is prevented or diminished by the prohibition of external signs, which, indeed, are more likely to serve as a reminder of what they signify. What is generally condemned under the name of ritualism is really ceremonial; for a rite consists in a

RITUAL

prescribed form of words; and what is meant is ritual for its own sake. But it might be replied that it is precisely Catholic worship that cannot be accused of ritualism, since it is believed the rite has symbolic significance and sacramental value. It is rather those growing areas of Protestantism where such rites as Baptism and the Lord's Supper are retained, while it is admitted that they no longer have clear necessity or definite meaning, which can be rightly charged with ritualism. At present, however, we can include under ritualism what is more properly called ceremonialism, returning to the question of prescribed prayers after we have dealt with the question of prescribed ceremonial.

Before we dicuss the general principles of ceremonial worship we must first deal with what would certainly be its sufficient condemnation, namely, that it is contrary to the express teaching and authoritative example of Christ. This ground of objection provides an illuminating example of how a whole literature can be carefully read and certain impressions carried away which, on examination, prove to be without any support whatsoever. For it is a fact, which anyone can verify, that Jesus never uttered a single word against the ritual observance of His own time. The significance of that silence is all the more weighty when we recall that Jesus was surrounded by a religion which practised an elaborate ritual, which not only regulated common worship, but extended over the details of ordinary life. It is true there was a complete difference between the worship of the Synagogue and that of the Temple, though, of course, there was no opposition between them. Nevertheless many expositors have argued that Christian worship took its rise rather from the Synagogue than the Temple. But it is interesting to observe that

RITUAL

while Jesus was accustomed to go to the Synagogue regularly, He also visited the Temple; and it was the Synagogue which eventually threw Him out, whereas He cast others out of the Temple. It must be remembered that the ritual of the Temple included the full Levitical sacrificial system, and yet we have no record that our Lord ever protested against it. In this He was unlike some of the prophets, who, in some of their writings, seem to be opposed to sacrifice on principle, and as not being of divine ordinance. Our Lord certainly quoted Hosea, speaking on this issue: " I will have mercy and not sacrifice "; but while Hosea may have been protesting against the sacrifices of the Temple, Jesus certainly was not, but only against the placing of regulations and prejudices before the call of human need. In His boyhood, according to St. Luke, Jesus found His way to the Temple, and was so absorbed in its interest that He quite forgot that His family might be concerned over His prolonged absence; and His reply to His mother's reproaches almost certainly means: " But surely you knew where to look for Me; Where should I be but in My Father's house ? " Whatever spiritual defect and decline may have characterized the Temple worship, our Lord recognized the Temple as His Father's house. Although the historicity of this incident has been questioned by the critics, it is by no means unlikely, since its attitude is confirmed by one of the most significant acts of His closing days, when, in indignation against the desecration of the Temple, He resorted to an act of symbolic violence. According to the popular estimate of our Lord's attitude, it might have been expected that He would have marched into the Holy Place and, like Cromwell, called upon the priests to " stop that fooling and come down." Instead of that He cleared the Gentile Court of the traffic which He regarded as desecrating the place, and especially because it prevented proselytes from joining in the services and finding there an undisturbed place of prayer. He forbade people using even the Outer Court as a secular thoroughfare. It was this action, so significant of His attitude, which helped to secure His condemnation.

It is true that our Lord demanded that religion must be inward and real, and that He condemned any outward act that was done for show or in hypocrisy; but He never taught that there must be no outward act, or dreamed that the one way of securing an inward and spiritual religion was by the easy method of abolishing external observances. One great saying of His lays down the broad and balanced principle quite clearly: "If thou art offering thy gift at the altar, and there rememberest that thy brother hath aught against thee, leave thy gift before the altar, and go thy way; first be reconciled to thy brother, and then come and offer thy gift." This saying recognizes that the offering of something to God at the altar may bring to remembrance a human duty left undone, and thus sanctions at least the mnemonic value of a rite. But although our Lord demands that the human duty must be discharged prior to the divine, so that the divine offering shall not be inconsistent, yet there is no suggestion that the human duty will suffice for the symbolic act of worship; the latter must still be performed when the other has been discharged. In addition to the ceremonial of common worship, the Jews practised numerous private observances and had added to them until they had become burdensome. Nevertheless our Lord observed these laws: if He ever

RITUAL

broke one of them He pleaded necessity, or recorded precedent; as in the case of an ox falling into a pit on the Sabbath Day or the historic instance of David and his men eating the shewbread. But normally He both kept the law Himself and advised others to do so. He commanded the cleansed leper to show himself to the priest; He paid the Temple tax even when He felt He at least ought to be exempted; and although He had a very low opinion of the moral consistency of the Scribes, nevertheless He commended obedience to their teaching while He commanded something superior to their example. The Pharisees had gone beyond the law in tithing such unimportant produce as mint, anise and cummin; but while our Lord condemned them for being so careful over matters like this when the weightier matters of mercy, faith and justice were neglected, He not only demanded that the greater matters should have been done, but also said that the others should not be left undone. When contrasting the Pharisee and the Publican at worship in the Temple, He condemns the one and praises the other; but it should be noted that it was the Publican who was the ritualist, for he stood afar off, and lowered his eyes, and smote upon his breast, in order to express the depth of his penitence. But we have not only our Lord's teaching to go by; we have also His own behaviour. Jesus submitted to the rite of baptism, an act which theologians have found it difficult to explain; for what need had He of baptism, or what could the ceremony have meant to Him? Yet He who knew no sin and needed no repentance underwent baptism; in contrast to some of His followers, who, with all the need in the world, have dared to excuse themselves from following His example and obeying His command.

RITUAL

It might be objected that here we have our Lord only condescending to convention lest He should raise false issues and excite unnecessary prejudice; but when we come to His own spontaneous actions we see that our Lord is still willing to use ceremonial and ritual expression. It has been confidently affirmed that no one could imagine Jesus taking part in a religious procession; whereas He not only took part in one, but Himself deliberately organized one as the only possible means of making His claims clear to the common people. Whatever it may be held that our Lord intended by the observance of the Last Supper, no one can dispute that it was a symbolic rite; it almost certainly followed the Passover, which He declared He had intensely desired to celebrate; or, if not, then some anticipated and similar, but still symbolic, ceremony; so that our Lord either added to an already ceremonial meal a further ceremony, or prescribed another ceremony to take its place. To those who maintain that our Lord only meant thereby that we should sanctify all meals by calling to remembrance His Presence, it must be replied that surely it would have been far better for that purpose if He had chosen some common meal, and one partaken of in the open air, instead of a symbolic meal which was only partaken of as a religious rite, and to which He added another of the same kind. This looks very like that elaboration of worship in which we are sometimes told Jesus had no sort of interest. But this attitude is all of a piece with His individual inclinations and His common observance. Although sometimes, when necessity demanded, He sat down to meat without the usual hand-washing, He no doubt astonished the Pharisee who invited Him to dinner when He complained that the usual ceremonies of courtesy had

RITUAL

been omitted; and to the perplexity of succeeding generations Jesus praised Mary's act of anointing at Bethany, which was not only an entirely symbolic act, but a very costly one. He praised it simply because of the affectionate devotion and spiritual insight that it displayed.

We can now turn to examine the actual principles of ceremonial worship. In one most significant and far-reaching statement Jesus laid down the principle that true worship must be " in spirit and in truth." As this statement was in reply to a question whether worship was to be at Jerusalem or Mount Gerizim, its immediate application is to discountenance national and ecclesiastical rivalry, and it certainly abrogates the centralizing of worship in one place. Does it, however, mean that worship must have no local expression, and that it must always be purely spiritual ? If to worship in spirit we must employ no outward forms, that means that not only must our bodies take no part in worship, but that we cannot worship properly until we are out of the body and have become pure spirits. But the principle laid down in the Fourth Gospel is only in accord with all that we have gathered from Christ's teaching in the Synoptics, namely, that whatever we do outwardly must be a true expression of our spiritual intention and desire; outward and inward religion must correspond. The New Testament is unanimous that by His own sacrifice Jesus abrogated the sacrifices of the Levitical system, but the institution of the Eucharist reveals His intention that His own perfect sacrifice was to be constantly commemorated. The new revelation demanded new modes of worship. Our Lord knew it was no use pouring new wine into old bottles, but neither did He believe that the new wine could dispense

RITUAL

with bottles altogether. The ancient rites must give place to new.

There are still, however, certain principles which must govern the employment of ceremony in Christian worship. Is elaboration or simplicity one of them? It will be admitted that some ceremony is necessary in all common worship, but it is sometimes maintained that it must be reduced to a minimum. For instance, it has been objected that a celebration, say, of High Mass, bears very little resemblance to the simple observance of the Last Supper in the upper room. Allowing for natural developments which must keep pace with historic growth and æsthetic culture, this difference is perhaps exaggerated. The descriptions of the Last Supper we possess are very compressed reports, but it can hardly have been so simple as some conclude. We are told that our Lord did certain things, such as blessing the bread and giving thanks, but these actions are not further described. If the Passover meal preceded the Lord's Supper, it was certainly accompanied by considerable ceremonial. Galilean peasants, as the disciples were, would almost certainly be wearing coloured garments, and quite likely special garments, since it was the custom to keep such for the Passover. The explanation of the seamless coat that our Lord was found wearing when He was arrested may well be that it was a garment that had been specially made as a gift to Him for this very ceremony. To reproduce the exact conditions of the first Eucharist, even if they could be recovered, would be a piece of merely antiquarian pedantry; while, on the other hand, it is more than likely that the ministers at the altar, vested after Catholic fashion, bear a closer resemblance to that first Eucharist than the appearance presented by some Protestant celebrations which have been

RITUAL

motived by a return to primitive simplicity. The Eucharistic vestments have been traced back by some to the ordinary dress of the Syrian peasantry, and by others to garments worn in the early days of the Roman Empire. Their retention serves the useful utilitarian purpose of avoiding personal eccentricity and individual variety in the celebrant's attire, which would be undesirable and distracting at such a time; it provides an opportunity for æsthetic expression which worship always craves; and symbolically confesses the Catholic belief concerning the Eucharist, and claims continuity with the historic and primitive Church, and communion with the saints and martyrs who have worn these same vestments in the same service.

If the question be raised whether ceremonial is necessary to the worship of God the answer must, of course, be " No "; none of our worship is necessary to God at all. If it be asked whether He prefers simplicity or symbolism, the issue is being confused, for it does not make for simplicity when all directions have to be given by the spoken or printed word, and where an atmosphere has to be created by explanations and exhortation. Vestments and posture, lights and incense, set forth far more simply than any other method what is intended and what is the feeling we ought to have at the Eucharist. God, who evidently delights in Nature's vestment of spangled stars and embroidered flowers, earth's perfume and the sunset's glory, can hardly be displeased when His children seek to express their joy and thanksgiving by methods that imitate His own creation. It is, of course, a fact that Catholic ceremonial took its rise from utilitarian necessity; certain things had to be done, and it was found that they had better be done uniformly, which would be less distracting both to celebrant and congregation.

RITUAL

The richness and elaboration of Catholic ceremonial also set forth the more all-embracing faith, the more assured convictions, the overflowing joy of Catholic worship; for it cannot be denied that the simplification of ceremony which Protestantism has demanded has coincided with a reduced significance of the Sacrament. But the utilitarianism of ceremonial covers more than the doing of outward acts in a certain way that shall be dignified and instructive; it arises from the fact that all common worship, if it is to have any expression, must employ ceremonial. However reduced it may be, the most Puritan form of common worship is bound to use some degree of ceremony. Even the Quaker meeting must be closed by the sign of the handshake; and to wear your hat at the meeting is as much a piece of ritual as to take it off in church. The Protestant efforts after greater simplicity have often produced only awkwardness or reintroduced ceremonies from secular life, while the absence of a guided ceremonial only overloads the service with verbal directions. Whatever can be said against the sensuousness of Catholic worship in the wearing of coloured vestments, the making of rhythmical movements, and the employment of such things as lights and incense, can be said with far greater force regarding the employment of music, the most emotional of all forms of artistic expression, which nevertheless Protestantism tolerates without apparently being aware of its dangers. And whatever can be said against using prescribed prayers, often composed by saints, can surely be said against the singing of hymns set to music, which has a definitely hypnotical effect and sweeps people into singing things of which they either know nothing or do not really desire to experience them. Yet in such matters it is recognized that danger cannot dictate disuse; and, indeed,

RITUAL

the provision of such aids may, and undoubtedly does, waken many from their complacency and indifference to become aware of their own spiritual longing, to make an attempt to attain the realities worship sets forth in symbol, and to express in their lives what they have professed with their lips.

On the other hand, Christian principles equally demand that ceremony shall never become a pretence, or be meaningless and burdensome. Therefore ceremonial must be always changing with growing thought and changing custom, though certain things will always remain the same, because they express more permanent elements in human nature, or set forth eternal realities. But we must be patient with this generation, for it must be remembered that the effects of Puritanism have robbed ordinary life of a good deal of its ceremony, and while this may be here, as well as in religion, really an unnatural repression, indicate a diminution of joy, and prove a discouragement of good manners and fine courtesy, it is useless to force upon people a ceremonial which has no meaning to them, which is distracting to their devotion or even excites their ridicule and contempt. Until we have a revival of religious conviction, the joy and fullness of the Catholic faith are rediscovered, and there is a general return to artistic expression in common life, which will make ceremonial more customary and natural, there should be provision for simple, spontaneous and almost silent services, in addition to the historic forms and the employment of full ceremonial. The contrast between Low and High Mass sufficiently sets forth and sanctions such a variety. Silent, corporate devotions before the Blessed Sacrament provide an example of how the one type of worship can prepare for the other; for, as some fear and others welcome,

RITUAL

such devotions will naturally pave the way for Benediction, a rite which only extends the adoration which has always been given to the sacred elements, and only uses what our Lord declared to be His Body for the purpose of blessing people as He Himself did when on earth. Benediction is deservedly popular because it combines impressive ceremony with the simplest of all religious worship; the adoration of God's glory and the quiet resting in His Presence. Catholic ceremonial, it must be insisted, came into existence in order to express the highest significance and the deepest feeling which the spiritual realities of worship demand and call forth; and even when the rite degenerates into vain or sacrilegious observance, it still proclaims its original significance, calls us to take hold of its inner reality, and condemns us for our irreverence, coldness and neglect. The provision of a type of worship that is devoid of any ceremony and is completely spontaneous, the spiritual value of which Protestantism has certainly helped to discover, can meantime stand alongside Catholic ceremony, and even be a training for its true observance, if only both are recognized to have their place and right within the Christian system.

Controversy about ceremonial is of all things most confusing and to be avoided, for it seems to concentrate upon what is secondary. It only does so because others are demanding that it has no place whatsoever. To those who are accustomed to ceremonial it is far more natural than using nothing but words; it provides for that joy and for those desires which pass beyond all possible expression in language; so that Catholic ceremonial really encourages that very inwardness which its critics often think can only be attained by the suppression of all outward observance.

RITUAL

The principles already discussed largely dispose of whatever objections can also be raised against ritual, using that word in its proper sense of the prescribed words which constitute a rite. The use of prescribed prayer in public worship is necessary if common needs are to be covered and individual desires and passing moods are not to become tyrannical. For this purpose prayers may be selected which were composed by masters of prayer and have proved their suitability by the test of time. But the prayers connected with the administration of a sacrament specially need to be prescribed, so that the intention of the sacrament shall be clearly expressed, and no one is left in doubt or in dependence upon individual interpretation. Liturgical prayer, as it is generally called, has, however, a certain conventionality about it. It must be keyed to an average level, its language must be restrained, it must be concise and yet suggestive. And all this may seem to some to impose fetters upon the free, familiar and spontaneous utterance which should characterize the communion of the soul with God. Jesus, nevertheless, recognized the need of a form of prayer when He taught the disciples "The Lord's Prayer." This was not intended to limit prayer to that form, but to provide an example of the widest and simplest possible form. But the peculiar purpose of liturgical prayer needs to be better understood. Its very form and style are intended to provide a starting-place, a general guide, or a summing up for individual, spontaneous and silent prayer. So in a devout congregation assisting at the Mass it may be noted that many are using books of private devotions, some are saying a rosary and some are lost in a type of prayer which has soared beyond the realm of words altogether. Yet both the ritual and the ceremonial

RITUAL

of the Mass provide such prayers with their inspiration, their common aim and their united offering, as well as serve to recall wandering thoughts and correct selfish petitions.

Prayers which alternate with a common and reiterated response may seem to the observer mechanical, and have been objected to as coming under our Lord's condemnation of vain repetition. But the discriminating " vain " is often overlooked. It is only the repetition of what is not meant that is condemned: for even in His awful agony we are told that Jesus could do no more than repeat the same words. In fact this very repetition serves not only to secure the attention of the congregation to what is being asked, but by its very nature engages the lower, mechanical side of the mind, and thus leaves the higher, mystical side free to explore the higher realms of prayer.

It will therefore be found that where liturgy is used, and its spiritual opportunity is realized, private devotion is encouraged and rare heights of prayer frequently attained; whereas where only extempore prayer is sanctioned, attention wanders and the individual prayer life tends to be sporadic, careless and undeveloped. This does not mean, however, that a liturgy need be limited and monotonous. There are vast masses of liturgical material that should be more widely known and made accessible for common use. Many of the saints have left us their own wonderful prayers, and these are specially suitable for inspiring and directing private prayer. But the normal use of prescribed prayers does not mean that extempore utterance should be condemned, or that simple gatherings for spontaneous prayer should be looked down upon. These are, however, most profitable when they are among folk familiar with one another,

RITUAL

when there is some specific need which makes prayer earnest, and also where the great forms of liturgical prayer have provided a guide, and silence is found to be equally eloquent.

Finally, in all ceremonial and ritual it must be remembered that it is a human expedient rather than a Divine necessity. God knows what we want before we ask, and better than we can express. But what is necessary to our human limitations and our common need our Father accepts. He does not need to be implored to grant us His mercy, yet because of what we are, and have been, we cannot take His mercy for granted; and so our prayers are always penitential. Yet it is through the voicing of our common needs and by the way of lowly, childlike prayer that He lifts us into higher communion with Himself, and through the worship that employs sacramental means makes His Presence most clearly known and felt. Therefore it is not surprising that, despite the prejudice which has accumulated against Catholic worship where it has been long disused, or the misunderstanding of its purpose has corrupted it by superstition; and despite the more popular appeal of Protestant worship, because it demands less understanding and entails less common agreement, Catholic worship is in principle and substance everywhere winning its way, while Protestant worship is manifesting its barrenness and insufficiency, and is now failing to attract the seeking spirit or express man's deepest needs.

X

THE CHURCH AND THE SOCIAL ORDER

IN face of the actual history and present condition of the Christian Church, it is difficult to frame any theory of the Church which is at once true to its foundations and to the facts of the existing situation, which will both satisfy spiritual ideals and cover historic developments; for any such theory seems to compel us either to accept a definition of the Church which places the majority of professing Christians outside the Church altogether, or to assume that the unity of the Church has been at least temporarily yet tragically destroyed. But when we turn to consider the relationship of the Church to the social order, any rigid and exclusive theory of the Church becomes still more impossible, for in the modern world those who are most concerned for the social life of mankind often either profess themselves Christian in faith and yet remain separated from the Church in any form, or declare themselves unable to hold the Christian faith completely or in any defined doctrinal sense, while perhaps claiming that they are nevertheless trying to carry out the teaching of Christ in its social application; whereas those most concerned about doctrinal and ecclesiastical Christianity often seem comparatively unconcerned about the social evils of mankind, are sometimes contemptuous of the social aspirations of the masses, and often hostile to all social reform. It is quite possible that this concentration of concern on the one side or the other is due to the specialization which seems inevitable with the modern mind, and that the opposition between institutional religion and organized reform is due mainly to misunderstanding and is capable of reconciliation; but that there is suspicion and even hostility between the general opinion and attitude of the Church as a whole and that of those anxious for social reform no one who knows the facts would dispute. However mistaken many social workers may be as to the real bearing of the Church's attitude, no one can doubt that there is a widespread belief either that the Church does not care about the conditions under which the masses labour and live, or that it is, for reasons which may be claimed to be spiritual, but which are suspected to be quite secular, opposed to the economic emancipation of the working classes. And for this once, however little it is cause for congratulation, we can use the word Church without any explanation or distinction; for whatever disagreement there may be among Christians as to where the true Church is to be found, or whom it includes, in the judgment of the class-conscious workers the Church, of whatever denomination, presents a fairly consistent complexion: Catholic or Protestant, Established or Free, the Church is not on their side, and is therefore against them. If a Churchman of any kind desired to represent the facts as otherwise he would perhaps call for some such distinction to be made before such a judgment were passed on the whole Church, but would thereby have to admit the existence of a very confused and anomalous state of affairs: first, a distinction between the Church's profession of sympathy for the condition of the people and its lack of practical aid in their struggle for emancipation; and, secondly, a distinction following the

THE CHURCH AND THE SOCIAL ORDER

more or less ecclesiastical complexion of various denominations, it being generally true that the more any communion exalts the ecclesiastical, the sacramental, the doctrinal, the less it seems to be concerned for the economic, the social, the material necessities of the people. For instance: it is Protestantism that has inspired and evolved the principle of political democracy, while Catholicism has generally been connected with autocratic or aristocratic government, and seems to prefer it; again, it has been the more decidedly Free Church denominations which have shown most sympathy with Labour ideals, while the Established Church of this country has in its general attitude, and particularly through its episcopal representatives in the House of Lords, until quite recent times, been almost consistently opposed to most social reforms. Roman Catholics will, however, hasten to point to the great Encyclical of Leo XIII on " The Condition of the Working Classes," in which the condition of the working classes is clearly recognized to be contrary to elementary justice, and certain principles are laid down which, if followed out, would no doubt bring considerable relief. But that same document, and Roman Catholic opinion generally, is nevertheless hostile to the programme of social reconstruction widely adopted by organized Labour under the general description of Socialism. To that important distinction we must return later. At present we have simply to recognize the existence of a fact, probably even more calamitous than the disunion of the Church, namely, the disunion of Christianity through the sundering of its dual concern for God and man.

There has emerged in our generation a conception of Christianity, which has become widely popular, that would dispense with definite doctrine or with

THE CHURCH AND THE SOCIAL ORDER

any serious concern for the Church, while yet maintaining that it is true to the most vital elements of Christ's teaching, because it is concerned for the material welfare of man and the establishment of a just order of society. It would be easy to show that this attitude can find no sanction in the New Testament and no support in the actual outlook of Christ, unless it is prepared to deny many of His sayings as unauthentic or regard His mind as at many points misled. It would also be easy to condemn this popular conception as a heresy, for that is precisely what it is, seeing that it simply takes that half of Christ's teaching which applies to the love of man and ethical conduct, and leaves out the love of God and all religious expression. But unfortunately the existence of this popular view can be largely traced to a reaction from the domination of a merely theological and ecclesiastical concern on the part of the Church, combined with the deplorable ethical example too often exhibited by the life of many ecclesiastics and the general failure to show any practical love for mankind. On the other hand, those who hold this popular conception and believe it to be the essence of Christianity need to be reminded that there is quite another attitude than theirs which is now gaining ground, namely, that Christianity is essentially an anti-social religion, and therefore is a positive hindrance to the establishment of a true social order, since it encourages individual concern for the salvation of the soul, and concentrates all hope upon the world to come; and this it is unwilling to dismiss as a misunderstanding of true Christianity, since it is the explicit teaching of the Gospels and can be traced to Christ Himself. Moreover, there is an even more extreme position gaining strength in the modern world, namely, that all religion, of whatsoever kind, is the

THE CHURCH AND THE SOCIAL ORDER

enemy of human welfare. It should be noted, therefore, that this dichotomy of Christianity into ecclesiastical and social only leads in turn to the more intense opposition between the worship of God and the service of man, until we arrive at a social theory which has for one of its essential and liberating principles the denial of God. In turn it is the existence of this extreme social theory envisaging a social order which can only be brought about by a violent revolution, combined with the repression of religion, and therefore threatening at the same moment the social and religious life of mankind, which has the effect, particularly on the Continent, of stiffening the Roman Catholic Church into opposition against Socialism as such, and tends to make most Christian people suspicious about any radical social reform as dangerous and most social concern as anti-spiritual. In this divorce between religion and reform, this opposition between the love of God and the love of man, this hardening antithesis of Christianity and Socialism, it is impossible not to see the menace of such a cleft in human outlook as must effectually prohibit all possibility of true social reform, paralyse all human hope, and, if it is allowed to deepen, bring upon mankind an unparalleled catastrophe.

In the presence of such confusion and suspicion it is difficult to thread a way to the truth or to attempt to state it without arousing prejudice, becoming embroiled in party strife, and losing oneself among economic controversies; and one of the chief difficulties of the situation is that we have so little authoritative guidance from the Church itself on this point to which we can appeal. This is because the subject of the social order is in many respects a new concern, for it is only within recent times that it has rapidly developed along lines that have exaggerated the iniquities and injustices which have always been prevalent in human society, but now so as to become intolerable and all-absorbing. Last century it was natural science, now it is economic theory that has disputed the place once given to theology. It is true that the developed theology of the Church, before it was challenged by Protestantism and forced to take a defensive attitude and upon narrower ground, regarded social theory as an essential part of theology, and scholasticism had outlined in the balanced elements of Private Property, the Just Price and No Usury, a general idea of great regulative value. It is easy to lay the blame for the destruction of this system and the hindrance to its being carried to further perfection at the door of Protestantism; but there were other and anterior courses at work. The development of finance to meet the demands of expanding trade and mechanical invention has gradually made the prohibition of the principle of usury impossible; the Church of the later Middle Ages by its extortionate exactions had itself belied the principle of a just price; and when the various movements of social protest have attacked the principle of private property, the Church has hurried to the defence of this remaining and now isolated principle, and thus not only has the wholesome balance of the mediæval system been overthrown, but the Church seems to have taken the field on behalf of a concern that is now suspected to be selfish, because it might touch the Church's large possessions, and, since it apparently defends private property without further definition, on behalf of a right which has accumulated immense possessions to the few, and left the many with hardly any property at all, has developed powerful monopolies which exercise an almost absolute domination over the lives of millions of men, and is not a right that is at least greatly insisted on in the Gospel. Nevertheless, Protestantism has even been blamed for the whole rise of the industrial, competitive and capitalistic system, because it has encouraged individualism, demanded freedom from all ecclesiastical interference in the secular realm, and has adopted belief in prosperity as a sign of God's favour. But the historic Catholic Church has been equally blind to the direction that economic development was taking, and until recent years gave no word of warning or counsel. And while Protestant concern for the social order, awakening earlier, has been inclined to attempt social reformation without reference to doctrinal foundations, and looking everywhere for help but to the inspiration of the Church's worship and the power of its organization; and while the enthusiasm for social reform has extended beyond the realms of the Protestant religion where humanitarianism has been made its only necessary basis, and Socialism has been put forward as a substitute for religion, the Churches, the more episcopal and the more Catholic they have been, the more they have been content to oppose the negative platitude that social reform is not enough, or to condemn Socialism outright as both a religious heresy and a social menace. We have to recall, moreover, that in this unfortunate and unnatural issue, when the service of man has been made a sufficient expression of Christianity, the Gospel does teach that at the Last Judgment the service of man will be recognized as the service of Christ; while the Epistles, of St. John in particular, give sufficiently explicit condemnation and denial of any profession of the love of God which does not carry with it the love of our brother also.

We cannot, however, rest content with attempting

to apportion the blame for this condition of things or with merely pointing out an unbalanced position. We want to try and discover what the true attitude of the Church should be towards social reform, and what, despite all blindness and blundering, the Church has actually done to inspire and direct it. And, in the first place, we must disentangle one of the great sources of our present confusion. We ought to be able to look to the Roman Catholic Church particularly to distinguish and to define, and its wholesale condemnation of Socialism has been too coloured by the continental type and temper of that movement, and overlooks the fact that Socialism is a broad and general name that now covers many degrees of socialization, various types of social theory, and quite conflicting methods for their realization. There is a large body of moderate socialistic opinion that embraces no principle and has no intention of putting an end to private property; while there can surely hardly be any large body of opinion, however conservative and opposed to revolutionary and extreme measures, that would deny the right or value of such a thing as public property. Therefore in defending the rights of private property the Roman Catholic authorities ought to define what property can properly be private, and to state why exactly the socialization of property should be regarded as sinful. All down the era of Christian history there have been various attempts to establish a system of common property. We have the record of such an attempt in the Acts of the Apostles, and if it must not be identified with modern theories of communism, it is certainly not to be assumed that the record has been preserved to us in order to show that it was a failure, and so that it should never again be attempted. It is a fact of considerable significance that the monastic orders, founded in order to carry out a more perfect practice of the counsels of the Gospels and to attain a higher sanctity, have always adopted the principle of common property. Various movements from time to time have arisen which have advocated the extension of this principle to the whole of society. Catholic opinion has resisted this proposal, first, because it was often founded on the doctrine that to possess any private property is a sin against the principle of Christianity, for which there is certainly no ground in the New Testament, but also because it was proposed to make into a coercive system what can never be anything but a voluntary principle. But while the distinction between the evangelic precepts and the evangelic counsels, particularly that of poverty, is theoretically sound, and must always be observed in passing moral judgments on others or in regulating what may be demanded from them, the following of the counsels is obviously to be encouraged, not only for the sake of those who would be perfect, but because of its regulative effect upon the whole of society. But this surely implicitly sanctions the principle that if society in general, through its democratic registration of opinion, consents to make certain property common, it has a perfect right to do so. It is true that the proposal to carry this out often raises the cry of confiscation, and confiscation is an offence against the commandment "Thou shalt not steal." But before this prohibition can be put into operation, it is necessary to inquire by what right people have already become possessed of what they now regard as their property, when it may be discovered that the commandment needs to be made somewhat retrospective in its action. What is called confiscation needs rather to be limited by considerations, first, of humanity to individuals, and, secondly, of financial stability. It is also true that many people who are passionate, nay, indignant for social reform are obviously motived more by the desire of revenge than justice, and more anxious to see the rich deprived of their possessions than concerned for any system which would materially raise the common level of distribution; and appeal often has to be made to that very avarice and cupidity which are the fundamental moral causes of our present social disorder in order to rouse enthusiasm for anything different. But moral theology teaches that the admixture of false motives does not entirely derogate from the value of the good; while the attractions offered to the avaricious have been sufficiently attached to the great offices of the Church, and yet this does not constitute a condemnation of the hierarchical system.

There is a sufficient and a growing body of opinion which is now aware that the precarious and sometimes destitute condition of what constitutes probably a third of our population is sheer injustice, and cannot be further tolerated without incurring the wrath of God upon our generation, and the endangering of the individual salvation of all those who are responsible for, or who acquiesce in, such conditions for their neighbours and brethren. It is not concern for individual salvation which can be held responsible for unconcern at these conditions, but a complete ignorance of what the conditions of individual salvation are. Moreover, it is surely nothing but common justice, and should not be beyond the capacities of civilization to secure that what is due to corporate or common enterprise shall be corporately owned and shared by all. It is the clamour of extreme theories that everything shall be so owned and organized which hinders calm consideration of what is rightly common property and should

THE CHURCH AND THE SOCIAL ORDER

be so administered; while the equally violent opposition to all public ownership is founded as much upon the fear of individual appropriation being hindered as of individual enterprise being sapped. There is a Christian Socialism, however, which depends first of all upon the seeking of the kingdom of God; that is, upon the sovereignty of God over the whole of life being recognized and visibly established. This has to be done by the application of the principles of justice; and surely there is no injustice in seeing that in the future the reward which has gone in disproportionate measure to individuals who have rendered little or no service shall be re-directed by a system of common ownership which shall secure common necessities for all the people. This principle is nothing more than an extension of taxation or the provision of public roads, which almost everyone recognizes as necessary and right. If it is objected that the slightest interference with individual profit-making is bound to decrease individual effort and so lower the general level of prosperity, the promise of the Gospel must be recalled, namely that when the kingdom of God and His justice are sought, all necessary things will be added. Even poverty is more tolerable when it is shared by everyone, and even in its lowest forms does not make for that denial of fellowship and, therefore, destruction of religion which always follow where the great inequalities of wealth and poverty produce fear and suspicion on the one hand, and envy and hate on the other. It is the injustice and inequalities of our present economic order which are the actual cause of so much of the irreligion which is characteristic of modern civilization, and this is confirmed by the fact that it is the middle classes who are now almost the last to practise and sustain religious observances. Here

THE CHURCH AND THE SOCIAL ORDER

are conditions, then, to which for every reason the Church ought to be alive, and there is surely a sane, evolutionary, progressive Socialism which contains absolutely nothing that could be regarded as in conflict with Christian principle, but, on the contrary, can be directly deduced from the great doctrines and sacraments of the Church. It may be found that in the interest of justice and of adequate distribution some things ought to be nationalized, others better municipalized, others, again, managed by voluntary co-operative enterprise, others by guilds of workmen owning and managing their own affairs; there would still be plenty of room left for all that can be better done by individual enterprise, and everything should be done by government and law to secure to all individuals that minimum of private property which is necessary to the protection of the human body, the production of food and the dignity of personality. It cannot be disputed that the communist idea derives its chief inspiration from Christianity, and the fact that it cannot be imposed by coercion does not mean that society should not be persuaded to adopt it voluntarily; and the fact that it has never been even approximately successful, save under the direction and discipline of a common well-defined faith, should not leave the Church content with condemning secular attempts. It is one thing to insist that without such a faith no extension of such a principle would ever be practicable, but quite another to denounce the ideal as in itself un-Christian because, in despair at the Church's apathy and the procrastination of professing Christians, men have turned to despotic coercion and the denial of Christianity as the only way of securing a communistic order.

When we go on to maintain that the Church has

THE CHURCH AND THE SOCIAL ORDER

always stood for a true social reform, it is obvious we have to use the word "Church" in a wider than its ordinarily defined ecclesiastical sense, for it must include not only the historic and Catholic Church, and all bodies who claim lineal and legitimate descent from it, but also that Church which has been defined as "the blessed company of all faithful people," which must include all those who even unconsciously draw their inspiration from Christ and are serving Him in His brethren, even though they would be the most surprised to learn it.

Nevertheless, it must be maintained that the Christian religion offers the only inspiration, Christian doctrine gives the only definite basis, and the Christian Church will prove to be the only organization that will finally produce and sustain a just social order. For it can be shown that the Christian Church, even as more rigidly and exclusively defined, has done more for social reform than any other body, and by its defined doctrines, its proclamation of the gospel and its dispensing of the sacraments is always serving, not only the glory of God and the eternal salvation of men's souls, but the redemption of society and the hope of the world, even when through temporary misunderstanding it fails all at once to see the social implication of its own principles and at times seems to be opposed to specific social reform or definite socialistic theories.

The primary task of the Church is to proclaim the supernatural basis and the supernatural end of human life. This, so far from being irrelevant to man's material needs and his temporal existence, must be given constant recognition and the first place in his concern if his common necessities are to be secured and his earthly life is not to become meaningless and intolerable, There will never be devised any system which shall secure economic justice unless it is founded upon the worship of God. If even humanity itself is proposed as the substitute for this, it will only degenerate in the end into a selfish struggle for material things; for these will seem the only good, and a superabundance of them will be sought in the vain attempt to comfort or stifle the soul which, with the denial of God, is left without companionship or satisfaction. Men seek more than they really need for their bodies, because they are striving also to satisfy their souls with that which never can. The consequence is gluttony and luxury, avarice and the lust of possession; and, since these can never be for all, superabundance in one direction means want and destitution in the other, while the working of the economic machine is in part deliberately directed, but for the most unconsciously functions to increase this disparity. The attempt to make it work more justly, by whatever system, will first of all be fought against by those who profit from its injustice, and even if they are defeated, it will only be kept operating justly by measures which will involve an immense bureaucracy and an enormous police force; for it will be an attempt to make a whole machine produce justice when its parts are directed towards injustice. The creation of a just social order needs the conversion of mankind both in mind and heart, and no appeal to economic principles or business methods, or even humanitarian sympathy, is capable of that task. The Church alone believes in the possibility of conversion -by divine grace, and it is the alternative of that or coercion by human tyranny which is all we have to choose from. It only needs that the Church shall preach the full gospel of divine charity expressing

THE CHURCH AND THE SOCIAL ORDER

itself in human redemption to effect this; but if human redemption is proclaimed apart from a divine purpose and saving grace, the Church is doing no disservice by spending all its strength in insisting on these as primary; in doing so it is concentrating its defence upon the citadel of all human hopes.

In recent years the policy has been constantly proclaimed or unconsciously pursued of concentrating upon man's temporal life and leaving his supra-temporal destiny out of account. Although partly done to redress the undue emphasis in the other direction, it is a short-sighted and fatal policy, has been of the greatest disservice to this present life, and its effects proclaim its mistake. Christianity and the cause of social reform as a result only find themselves both confronted by a vast mass of people who either live for selfish pleasure and are deaf to all idealistic appeals, or are too hopeless to believe that anything can be done with a world which, on the secular hypothesis, is so meaningless in its entire lack of purpose, developing personality as it does with infinite effort and by such pain only to destroy it. Moreover, the making of this life the only concern and the final end of man loads reforming zeal with the impossible task of trying to make this the perfect world instead of the preparation for it. So social reform is previsaged on a scale that can never be realized, namely, to make a temporal scheme that will satisfy all man's desires; and thus its proposals are laughed out of court from the outset by those who do not desire even their partial success; whereas the true connection between this life and the life to come enables man to endure the discipline and toil of earthly existence that are essential to its purpose, while it compels men to seek justice here on earth for their fellows,

THE CHURCH AND THE SOCIAL ORDER

because only by that means can they qualify for the Kingdom of Heaven and secure a place in the communion of saints.

The proclamation of the essentially supernatural character of human life and destiny is therefore the Church's indispensable contribution to the social order, and, even if it were the sole contribution, is sufficient to justify the place the Church claims in men's regard and loyalty; and the worship and the sacraments of the Church keep alive the sense of the supernatural, while declaring that its power is realized through the consecration of the natural order and the sanctification of material things. The persistence, the unity and the extension of the Church should therefore be the primary concern of all who profess themselves humanitarians, philanthropists, reformers, or socialists.

XI

THE CATHOLIC CHURCH AND INTERNATIONALISM

INTERNATIONALISM is, so far as language goes, almost a perfect translation in modern terminology of what Catholicism originally meant. For Catholic, as we have shown previously, is a term that, when first coined, simply meant "throughout the whole (world)"; and it came into use as an appeal to the belief and practices of the Church as a whole as against local and sectarian movements. "The whole world" of those early days was, however, only the world embraced by and known to Mediterranean civilization. But so soon as ever the Church became aware of the world outside those narrow confines, it extended its outlook and concern to embrace its farthest limits; for its catholicism was implicit from the beginning. Its original charter was to make disciples of all the nations; its final ingathering had been seen in prophetic vision to include "a great multitude, which no man could number, out of every nation, and of all tribes and peoples and tongues"; and St. Paul had declared that in Christ Jesus mankind had found a unity which transcended all physical, racial and national divisions. The Church, then, in its constitution and nature, is essentially international; it is more, it is supra-national; it does not merely spread beyond national barriers as if they did not exist, nor does it attempt simply to break them

THE CATHOLIC CHURCH

down; it subsumes them in a higher unity by means of a profounder loyalty, because it proposes unity not in a higher abstraction, but in a supreme, all-embracing and reconciling Personality, Christ Jesus.

A time soon came in history when racial and national considerations began to oppose themselves to the claims of the new brotherhood, but whenever this opposition developed the Church immediately claimed the superior loyalty. This was the issue discerned and determined by the Apostle Paul in the first great conflict within the Church between Jew and Gentile; for the apostle saw that the demand that to become a Christian, a man must first virtually become a Jew, was to make Christianity subservient to something that was purely racial. The next opposition to develop was that between the Roman Empire and Christianity. The actual issue was somewhat confused by the demand for an expression of loyalty to the Empire that involved idolatry, to which, of course, no intelligent and consistent Christian could for a moment yield. And what sharpened the issue to an impossible point was the corollary demand that the Christian should curse Christ. But behind this there must have been something more than a stupid blunder on the part of the Imperial authorities in attempting to exact a renunciation of a new religion and another deity; for, providing the divinity of the Emperor was recognized, Rome had no objection to admitting swarms of new deities. It must have been perceived, however unconsciously, that there was something in the claims of Christ which challenged the absoluteness of Imperial loyalty. It was not simply that absolute and sole Godhead was claimed for Christ: the Jews had made the same claims for Jehovah; but Christ's absoluteness extended to earthly rule as well as to heavenly worship: He was the King of kings as well as Lord of lords; and on all matters concerned with this world the Empire felt it necessary to be supreme. The martyrs died in their thousands rather than consent to the recognition of the divinity of the Emperor or the worship of his image. But, as we can now see, they were dying for a principle that carried far more than perhaps many of them recognized, namely, the supremacy of religion above all earthly concerns, even above what was regarded necessary by pagan politicians to secure the stability of the State. After the adoption of Christianity as the religion of the Empire, consequent upon the conversion of Constantine and his accession to the Imperial throne, the conflict entered upon a stage of confusion which to this day has never been cleared up. The claims of the Church became more and more for an absolute supremacy, even extending to the right to crown kings and to relieve nations from their allegiance to their monarchs if they rebelled against the Church.

The constant strife between Church and State thus begun has gone on until our day. It may be thought that this was due simply to the failure to recognize the line of demarcation between them. The State was constantly transgressing beyond its legitimate sphere by attempting to interfere with the government of the Church or the appointment of its officers. On the other hand, royal persons and State officials felt that the Church had often exceeded its rightful authority and had attempted to interfere with purely secular or legal affairs. But the ultimate cause of the quarrels was that the Church claimed a supreme authority from

THE CATHOLIC CHURCH

which it believed all other authority was derived. In the Middle Ages attempts were made to ease the conflict not only by marking out the boundaries of the two spheres, but some religious and political thinkers, such as Dante, proposed the solution that the power of the State was derived directly from God and not immediately through the Church. So the working theory has come to be adopted that the Church's rights extend only over the spiritual, and those of the State only over the temporal affairs. But in actual practice it constantly proves very difficult to determine where the one ends and the other begins, and the theory has by no means given us a solution of the problem. The confusion was added to by the fact that the Church soon became not only very wealthy, but the largest corporate landowner; and its financial management favoured not only exactions, but corruptions. And, worst of all, the Papacy became a temporal princedom, and so not only sought the protection of the temporal sword, but itself directly employed it. So the true point of conflict, namely, between the Church's internationalism and nationalistic claims, was concealed, and has remained so even in our own day.

There can be little dispute that whatever part was played at the Reformation by the concern for a purer, simpler and more spiritual religion, the uprising of national feeling also played some part in the rebellion against the Papacy; and, as a consequence, in many of the reformed countries religion was delivered over to the decision of rulers and placed under the direction of the State. Owing, however, to the combination in the mediæval Papacy of the extension of temporal power with the discrediting of its spiritual prestige, the issue between the spiritual internationalism of the Church and the secular nationalism of the State was again confused and was almost completely undiscerned. Consequently, one of the results of the Reformation was undoubtedly the exaltation of nationalism and the creation of an absolutist State.

It has taken four hundred years to discern the enormous dangers to humanity that lie in these conceptions. The resurgent spirit of nationalism has not only broken the comity of nations and brought Europe to a welter of blood and carnage, but it manifests such intransigeance that it refuses submission not only to any spiritual power, but often to any secular international arrangement that would be for the benefit of the whole, or to any compact that would prevent the nations from going to war. This nationalistic spirit helps to manufacture contempt for other nations and prompts the insane ambition to conquer them. At the present moment it is not only still keeping the Western nations in deadly fear of one another, but it is raising up national movements of still more gigantic proportions and most fearful portent in the rest of the world outside, particularly in the East. We have also recently had indications that a communistic State can become absolutist and then violently atheistic, and that is probably the general and inevitable tendency of the absolutist State. The historic Catholic Church, all down history, has therefore been fighting the supreme battle for the liberty of the individual and for the unity of mankind; and down beneath many of the confused issues of the hour the Roman Catholic Church, however unconsciously to itself and unapparent to outsiders, is still standing for a true internationalism, and so remains the last protection of the individual soul against the

THE CATHOLIC CHURCH

enslaving demands of the modern State. But it will be found that nationalism very rarely rises to any vivid consciousness or passionate outburst save when a nation has been threatened with dictation or slavery by another. The nationalistic element in the Reformation would not have played the part it did if, first, the Roman See had not long been attempting to assert an authority over the temporal affairs of the nations, and secondly, it had not itself become nationalized. Although the world-wide mission of the Catholic Church has been nobly sustained by the Roman See since the Reformation by its self-sacrificing and often martyred missionaries (though in that it has been equalled, and perhaps outstripped, by the missionary efforts of the Protestant Churches), and although the temporal claim of the Papacy has practically been abandoned or transformed into the perfectly legitimate demand for a minimum of extra-national territory, an Italianate Papacy and a predominantly Italianate Curia give a colouring to the Roman Church which is national rather than international; and where the Reformation has long held sway, not only are the claims of the Roman Church felt to be a danger to national liberty, for which history certainly gives some ground, but its organization looks like involving subservience to an alien authority, while many of its customs in worship seem foreign and exotic. On the other hand, the political entanglements of the Roman Church, even in countries less touched by the Reformation, often cause the Church to side with and to intensify the nationalistic spirit; so that in some countries it is the Catholics who are the greatest opponents to international understanding, whether its motive is socialistic or purely pacific. In Protestant countries, where the Roman Church is under suspicion as an alien, it often seems to become ultra-patriotic in order to give no colour to this suspicion. It is therefore a fact hardly to be disputed that the Church which, by its claim to be the Holy Catholic Church, ought to be the chief support of internationalism, by a series of unfortunate historical happenings and political confusions is doing nothing like what it ought to be doing for internationalism ; in fact, in the judgment of some who are labouring for internationalism, it is one of the greatest hindrances.

Some excuse for this failure of the Catholic Church can, however, easily be found in the mixed character and dubious motive of a good deal that passes for internationalism. There is an internationalism that prefers to talk vaguely about loyalty to humanity as a whole, simply in order to find an excuse for not doing one's immediate duty to one's own nation ; there is an internationalism which is motived solely by commercial considerations and the hope of financial gain. But to come to deeper principles, it could be rightly objected that the real principle of Christianity does not propose the abolition of nationality, for it is obvious that God has trained the world through the creation of racial and national entities, and that such things, for instance, as a world State, a universal language, or a single type of culture, however attractive and easy a solution they seem, would really diminish the corporate riches of humanity and give us instead something that is merely diffuse, diluted, monotonous and of a lower average level. In Christ nationality and race are transcended, not abolished, and in the Catholic Church nationality need not be abolished, any more than to attain national unity the family must be abolished.

Again, the internationalism which the modern world is now striving to attain is perforce secular; the religious divisions of mankind, and the unwillingness to admit the claim that there is one true, supreme religion, make it impossible to seek unity on a religious basis. The nationalistic instinct is easily aroused against the supreme claims of the Roman Catholic interpretation and administration of Christianity. It was a curious but significant fact that during the Great War a secret treaty should have been drawn up between Great Britain, France and Italy to exclude the Papacy from any part in the negotiations or settlement of peace. No doubt this action in the main only indicates the completely secular outlook of modern statesmanship, but it also indicates with what suspicion the Papacy is even now still regarded; and who can say there have been no historic reasons that have given rise to that suspicion? And if internationalism is now so often secular, is that not to be charged in part to the failure of the Catholic Church to proclaim and establish the true internationalism?

The attitude of the historic Catholic Church towards internationalism is, however, felt by many purely pacific internationalists to reach the point which makes it a hindrance rather than a help in its unsatisfactory attitude towards war. There can be no doubt that, along with much that is still militant and belligerent, there is a growing pacific spirit throughout the world; and either through the disillusioning experience of actual warfare, through a growing idealism, or because of further study of the New Testament and the teaching of the Early Fathers, the more definite doctrine of "pacifism" is taking hold. Pacifism is the theory that the taking up of arms is a sin against humanity, contravenes the commandment " Thou shalt not kill," and is condemned by the teaching of Christ. Against this the attitude of the Roman Church remains attached to the scholastic idea that war can be just, on the principle that a man has a right to defend his property or his life, and therefore nations their prosperity, freedom or existence when they are attacked by an aggressor. This doctrine is probably not *de fide*, but it is traditional, and it certainly secures the support of the majority of Roman Catholic theologians, and, for once, the other Churches and the world are on their side.

At this point some notice should be taken of the almost solitary and sustained protest of the Society of Friends, who hold that the bearing of arms is forbidden to the Christian. The fact that this tenet is held by a body of Christians who are in many respects the farthest removed from Catholicism in their repudiation of a sacerdotal priesthood and in their complete abandonment of the sacraments of the Church induces some people to suspect that the organization, doctrine and practices of Catholicism are by this one consideration sufficiently condemned; they have to be abandoned to recover liberty to find the truth and follow Christ. On the other hand, those who believe in the one Church, the apostolic succession, and sacraments may be equally inclined to dismiss pacifism as a heresy, just because it is usually found associated with bodies farthest removed from Catholicism. But the matter obviously calls for a more careful distinction. There are those whose pacifism does not include a condemnation of all war as sin, because they would only regard the participation in war as sin in the case of the person who had a conscientious objection to taking

THE CATHOLIC CHURCH

part in it. And the Quaker witness is actually founded on such a conviction. It is not so much to proofs taken from texts that they look for the sanction of their convictions, but to the inner light granted to the individual soul. And the Society of Friends, by its constitution and spirit, does not claim to be the whole Church, and could be included in a Catholic system as really intending to be nothing more than an order within the Church, seeking, through fellowship, to attain interior illumination, and conceiving it as part of their vocation not to bear arms. Moreover, there are those who believe that the way of breaking the menace of war will never be found by treaties, leagues, or other attempts to make war legally impossible, but only by the determination, on conscientious grounds, by ever greater numbers, to take no part in war, and to abide by the consequences, whatever they be. And certainly their numbers are bound to grow.

Now is there anything in the defined doctrinal position of the Catholic Church that condemns this kind of pacifism? On the other hand, is there not much in its practice which actually sanctions it? It can certainly be claimed that the issue is by no means dogmatically settled in the Roman Catholic Church, despite the expressed condemnation and contempt of certain individuals for such a position; for, and however slowly, the pacifistic element even there is making itself felt, and the claim for the ecclesiastical sanction of the refusal of the individual to bear arms will be heard more of as years go by, and will have to be met by other arguments than those favoured by secular politicians and ruthless militarists. The very fact that by Canon Law the priest is not allowed to shed blood, and monastics claim exemption from bearing arms (although, in the Great War, under the pressure of some secular governments, they were temporarily released from their vows), it is obvious that an individual vocation that includes the refusal to bear arms thereby receives high sanction, and it is difficult to see what condemnation there can be for others who, at the bidding of their conscience, or by their desire to attain spiritual perfection, feel they cannot take up arms without sin.

From the point of view of traditional doctrine, and of finding room therein for a personal conviction on this subject, it is obvious that everything turns upon the question of right. If it is right for a man to possess private property, it is also right for him to defend it; he has a still greater right to defend his own life or the lives of others; and therefore it must be maintained that there is such a thing as a just war. But under the conditions of modern diplomacy the decision as to what constitutes a just war cannot be left any longer to governments, or even to national instincts; for we have discovered that under such conditions every war will seem or be made to seem just to every nation that takes part in it. The traditional theory, left further undefined, therefore gives practical sanction to all wars for ever. An attempt is being made to define a just war as one of defence, and an unjust war as one of aggression. But modern circumstances make it impossible to decide who is actually the aggressor, at least until long after the war is over; and it is an accepted axiom of military policy that the best method of defence is aggression, if there is any reason to believe that some other nation is preparing for hostility. Now while it may be admitted that private property and self-defence are natural rights, it may well be asked whether the one is the way of perfection, or the other is the way of charity. The complete disproof that war now brings any advantage to the victor, secures any of the idealistic aims for which it is waged, or gives any guarantee of permanent peace, or that preparation for war does anything but incite and hasten it, is now being borne home upon the thoughtful of all nations. But these are still merely temporal and prudential considerations. It is certain that with the growth of individual liberty and judgment there will be found in the future ever-increasing numbers of people (and the greater numbers in those countries where there is more freedom and education), who will refuse to take any part in war, for whatever reasons. The Roman Catholic Church cannot contemplate the task of persuading these people, in the name of Christ, that it is their duty to kill their fellows, at the bidding of secular governments, in the wholesale and murderous fashion of modern warfare, with all its accompaniments of lying, spying and slanderous propaganda. It is not a question of the private interpretation of Scriptural texts, but a question of vocation and the consideration of charity, and on that issue the Roman Church is pledged to sanction individual abstention from war. Now it is certain that any open sanction of this attitude would bring the Roman Church into still graver disrepute among the secular-minded nations; but it would be here, at least, for indisputably Christian reasons, to her everlasting honour, and with the approval of posterity. This type of Christian pacifism, therefore, does not need to contravene the doctrine that war may be just, or to hold that war has never done anything for humanity; neither need it be made a corollary of this attitude that private property must be denied. It is rather a question whether a man may not be driven to surrender his private property, and to give up his own life, if the only means of defending either is the taking of someone else's life under the methods of modern warfare. This position does not involve the condemnation of all use of force in the exercise of public justice, for in that case we have the fair trial and free verdict which war never gives; though it certainly might be taken to involve the question whether public justice has the right to take another person's life. The right of inflicting the capital penalty is being gravely questioned, and has already been abandoned in some European countries, some of them Catholic countries. If individual pacifism can alone break war; and this seems in line with the way of the Cross and the martyrs, and to promise similar effects, then the Roman Catholic Church, because of her still international character and her wide authority, holds the key to the situation. Shall it be said that, like the lawyers of old, she took away the key of knowledge and entered not in herself, and them that were entering in she hindered?

Behind this issue it is now evident there lies the old question of the supremacy of the Church over the State. That supremacy, it is now recognized, must depend not upon anything temporal or coercive, but on something wholly voluntary and spontaneously loyal, and, as Catholicism spreads, as in the future it must, by individuals being converted from pagan nationalism, then, in virtue of belonging to the Church, the true international, and of the potential inclusion of all mankind in the Church, a loyal Catholic may rightly refuse to shed his brother's blood. Meantime for Protestants the indisputable Scriptural doctrine of

THE CATHOLIC CHURCH

the royal priesthood of all believers might well apply to that wider priesthood, the Canon Law of the Catholic Church concerning the sacerdotal priesthood. For just as the Catholic Church will recover its sway over humanity as it completely disentangles itself from political intrigue, and looks solely to the spiritual weapon of persuasion and intelligent obedience to its supreme claim to loyalty, so, it may be predicted, will the menace of war be finally broken, not by superior preparation and threat of hostilities, but by individual refusal to fight and the voluntary disarmament of the nations.

Such a pacifism cannot be commended to others until they see that it is a counsel their conscience bids them follow; nor can it be commended to vast numbers of mankind until they have accepted the Christian valuation of all things, for that, on issue, demands not only that the individual life, but this world and all its concerns, must be surrendered for the sake of the possession of eternal life. It is therefore to the Catholic Church that we shall still have to look for a truly spiritual internationalism, although it will have to be to the Catholic Church only when it has determinedly, openly and dogmatically turned its back for ever upon some of the errors and entanglements of the past, and has become a Church whose supremacy will be acknowledged because it is purely spiritual, and is therefore seen to be the only possible basis upon which the unity of humanity can be attained or international peace preserved.

The last great battle for Christianity must be fought in this world unarmed, and free from every kind of external coercion. It does not matter if the issue of the battle be in doubt; the victory will remain with the Church, as it remained with

Christ, even though the Church, like Him, be put to death.

And there is the more reason to hope and pray that the Catholic Church may have its eyes opened to this task and be encouraged to this adventure, first, because it will do more for the real reunion of Christendom than any amount of negotiation; the atmosphere will at last be cleared and the issues clearly seen, and the truth will rally to its banner the loyal who are willing to take up the weapons of love. But, secondly, the establishment of the true, spiritual International will save us from the dreadful alternative of a wholly secular International; for all present tendencies show that a secular internationalism is bound to become not so much idealistic and humanitarian, as economic and coercive. For there is in construction another International in which the proletariat of the world aims at throwing off in every country the chains of the present industrial system, and, to achieve its end, will disown national patriotism, and seek to create a new internationalism, at first simply secular and non-religious, but in the end almost certainly bound to become atheistic and anti-religious. The activities of this International will one day probably paralyse some attempt of the nations to go to war, but only too probably to establish another kind of war, horizontally between the classes instead of perpendicularly between the nations; and if they gain the victory, as, if they know how to use their strength they can, they will march to it through seas of blood and establish it by an iron law of tyranny. It is all too apparent that the fine idealism of the Labour movement, and the persuasive methods of evolutionary Socialism, may through impatience with the Church and in the absence of religious faith end in a recourse to coercion and the attempt at a communistic revolution. But it must be remembered that the nightmare of such an internationalism will be largely chargeable to the abandonment by Christendom of its own glorious dreams; and the belief in the shedding of blood, and the violent overthrow of society which will be necessary, will be able to appeal to the one-time sanction of the Catholic Church of a just war and the murder of the tyrant; coercion will be resorted to because it will seem the only alternative to conversion; and such a conversion, which might have been brought about by the Church proclaiming the brotherhood of mankind in the Kingdom of God, that, for the sake of such a Gospel, men would have given up all they possessed to find perfection, and have listened to Christ's command to put up the sword in order to embrace the nobler weapon and only redeeming way of the Cross.

XII

THE CHURCH AND HUMANITY

IT is notorious that ecclesiastical questions are apt to become absorbing, and, because of this, to produce a narrowing of concern; and this never more so than when we are faced, as we are to-day, with such differences of opinion as to the nature of the Church and its identification, involving Christendom in continual controversy, competition and strife. This unfortunate tendency must not, however, be allowed to dictate the conclusion that ecclesiastical questions are about things that do not matter, which is the judgment constantly passed upon them when they absorb interest and energy, and thus draw good men's minds from the crying needs of humanity, namely, the provision for the common necessities of life, social justice and international peace. Fortunately it is now being widely recognized that the divided condition of Christendom is an intensely practical question, for it means the absorption and waste of spiritual energy, and the Church cannot serve humanity properly unless it is at peace with itself. But if the Church is to uphold the supreme concern of ultimate truth and united worship, it must not degenerate into a merely secular agency for the relief of the temporal needs of mankind. The very purpose and existence of the Church depend upon the belief that it is not enough to relieve mankind's temporal needs: man has other needs as clamant and painful, and the Church holds that man's temporal needs have now become such a burden and present so absorbing a problem, simply because the ultimate truth about humanity has been forgotten or denied, and corporate worship has been broken up by individualistic preferences, and is neglected for less important claims or for the pursuit of selfish pleasure.

The concern, however, of the Church to defend its necessity, and its preoccupation with the divisions of Christendom, are naturally liable to make the Church present the appearance of being concerned only with itself, and there is a type of well-intentioned ecclesiastic who, in zeal for the Church's unity and welfare, seems to forget why it is essential that these should be secured. To prevent this perversion the Church is urged by advisers from within and by critics from without to remember that it is not an end in itself; it exists solely to carry out the purposes of God and to serve the highest interests of humanity. If these ends are lost sight of, the Church would become more than useless; it would become a hindrance, a nuisance, and a source of corruption. But not only by its very faith and form, by divine promise and protection is it held that it will never succumb to decay or death, but it can be held that the Church is an end in itself. The Church is really the end of humanity, and not humanity the end of the Church; since it is by humanity being united together and to God that its end is fulfilled, and the Church is nothing else but the realized union of mankind in God. Nevertheless, the Church can only flourish in proportion as its own true end in itself is kept in view, and all its efforts and concerns are directed to the realization of that end. It would not, however, do to regard the Church as merely an organization which consists of individuals and exists for their sakes: it is an organization which exists for the sake of creating an organism; that is, such a relationship of individuals as creates a new kind of organic structure, a spiritual body on whose functioning the spiritual life of individuals depends. The Church is thus the only community that can be rightly personified, not only because it is a body which has a living personal head, Christ, who is the head of His body, the Church, but it can also be referred to as a person, namely, Christ's Bride, the Wife of the Lamb. The purpose of the Church is to bring individuals into union with God; but if there is to be real union and of deep enough capacity, there must be not only many individuals to participate in that union, but they must first be knit together in a very close union with one another, if any one of them is ever to attain profound and satisfying communion with God. The Church is therefore necessary for the highest human experience; it is necessary to fulfil the purpose of God, which is to bring humanity to the fullest possible union with His nature, mind and glory. The Church, therefore, when compared with individuals, is an end in itself; it is only when compared with God that its end is not in itself but in Him.

Nevertheless, the complaint is made against the Church that this conception of its nature and function has made it both exclusive and anti-humanitarian. The Church is not wide enough to embrace the whole of humanity, because it demands submission to certain beliefs as a condition of membership; and in the present confusion of thought and the questioning of all intellectual concepts, it is felt that the Church is not only falsely exclusive, but is bound to become confined to an ever smaller number of persons in the modern and the future age. The attempts, however, to widen the doorway or to set up a different kind of test can hardly be said to provide any hope of meeting this complaint. The Catholic Church stands for exacting the maximum faith; candidates must believe all that the Church proposes for belief. In revolt from this, there have been various attempts to discover a less exacting standard in the various Confessions of the Reformed Churches. But the earlier attempts only provoked further intellectual revolt, while the later attempts tend to become more and more vague and capable of being taken with undefined reservations, until in some bodies the demand for any declaration of belief is declared to be a difficulty by people who profess themselves to be sincerely religious and desirous of belonging to the Church. Some of the Reformed Churches turned from the exaction of any belief, but only to demand an assurance of being predestined, or of having passed through some satisfactory religious experience. The former of these tests has now been abandoned, and even the latter has become for the modern mind too stereotyped and narrow and too encouraging of inquisition on the one side and insincerity on the other. There have been tentative modern proposals for making a purely ethical profession sufficient, such as the desire to serve humanity in the spirit of Jesus Christ. But there are signs that it is felt necessary to accompany the diminution of the demand for belief by some assurance of ethical behaviour, such as a general reputation for respectability, or even an assurance upon certain specific points of conduct that many feel to be ethically disputable or ethically superficial.

In contrast to these adaptations of Protestantism to modern demands, the Catholic Church holds that it is its duty still to maintain its witness to man's profoundest need, and to the whole truth on which the satisfaction of that need must rest. To give way on a single point of faith would be to

THE CHURCH AND HUMANITY

imperil the whole, and without faith there is no hope of satisfying human need. It is now becoming an acute practical question whether anything is actually gained by reducing this demand or by altering the basis on which the Catholic Church makes it, namely, that the whole faith as taught by the Church must be believed, and because the Church believes it. For any reduction of the various items to be believed leaves some which are just as intellectually difficult to some people; and if a person does not believe in the Church, how can he sincerely wish to enter an institution he does not believe in or dare not trust on the highest issues? The Protestant Churches in one sense demand more intellectual belief than the Catholic Church, because, however much fewer may be the beliefs demanded, those that are retained are no less difficult than those that have been rejected, for the latter were simply dependent upon the former; and since nothing is accepted by the Protestant on the authority of the Church, each person must select and believe every doctrine solely on his own rational conviction.

The Catholic Church maintains that the charge of indifference to the needs of humanity, such as physical insufficiency, bodily suffering or political subordination, is not fair to the facts of history when there is borne in mind her immense philanthropy, to which her children have been constantly inspired, her repeated condemnation of injustice, and the fact that the worth placed upon the individual soul by the Christian religion is the sole intelligible sanction for democracy. This alleged indifference only exists in the minds of those who are confident that only on certain social theories can everyone's need be guaranteed a supply, whose concern for physical suffering makes it the supreme

THE CHURCH AND HUMANITY

evil with which mankind is afflicted, and who believe that political enfranchisement alone is all that is necessary to effect the redemption of mankind. This mere humanitarianism, the Church maintains is superficial, would prove anything but satisfying, and, as a matter of fact, would do the greatest harm to humanity. On this ground the Roman Catholic Church has been willing to defend even the religious persecutions of the past, for it maintains that the physical suffering of such a dreadful ordeal as being burned alive is not for one moment to be weighed against the danger of untrue belief; for untrue belief, in the end, is bound to bring upon humanity not only mental pains of despair, depression and doubt, but all kinds of physical evils, such as civil war, disease and starvation. It would certainly augur better for the health of the modern mind if its objection to the persecutions of the past, sanctioned by the Church, were due not so much to horror at the infliction of pain as to the harm it has done to religion; and that, not only because of the people who have been kept from belief in the Church because it has sanctioned such methods, but because of the people who may have professed a faith that was due only to coercion or fear.

The Church can well defend the attitude of its dominant concern by maintaining that the faith it holds it holds for the future and for the good of all humanity; and indeed there can be no assurance, even in the present confusion, that the Church will fail to secure the allegiance of the modern intellect when once it has emancipated itself from some of its ill-founded arrogance, its unexamined dogmas, and its imaginary difficulties. Again, the Catholic Church may well maintain that it keeps its limits so rigidly defined because it wants to convey to humanity an undiluted grace and an undiminished assurance; and it would be impossible to hold wide hopes for individuals now, or for humanity as a whole in the future, if the Church's rigid principles did not guarantee that the treasures of the Church would be available to all ages, and are in no danger of being bartered away to meet some temporary and superficial need.

Nevertheless, it has surely become obvious to enlightened Churchmen of all kinds, and not least to those of the historic Catholic Church, that there is all the difference between maintaining a position in merely extreme and unexplained opposition to the demands and needs of men, and showing how it is the Church's position which really contains what they are seeking; there is all the difference between denying that bodily sufficiency, physical health and social freedom are all that man requires, and, in order to oppose those who make them the sole concern, giving them no real or insufficient attention; and especially is there all the difference between maintaining the faith unchanged, and in failing to show how the intellectual difficulties of the modern world are not increased, but rather diminished by the Catholic faith, and how the wide welcome of such faith would be the surest solvent of all human evils. And it is especially necessary to explain how it can be that the determination of the Catholic Church to maintain its faith undiminished and its borders defined does not conflict with its mission to all mankind, and does not deny, but sanctions, the hopes that may be held concerning those who are outside the Church, and far outside the Christian faith. For these hopes can only be held because the Catholic Church holds the revelation of God's love and justice, and maintains the efficacy of Christ's sacrifice for the sins of the whole world.

THE CHURCH AND HUMANITY

It is at this point that an illuminating and liberating idea can be brought into play from the undisputed, but often misunderstood, relationship held to exist between the organized visible Catholic Church and the Mystical Body of Christ. It is not Catholic doctrine that they are one and the same. The organized and visible Church is only the sacrament of the invisible Church, and at any time may be a very imperfect sacrament of it. Moreover, it is the Mystical Church that is the source of all power and salvation. This belief has certain quite practical conclusions. In the first place it involves the admission that many who are not only enrolled in the visible Church but are partakers of its visible sacraments are not members of the Mystical Church at all, because they are really unfaithful to their light and opportunity. They are the tares that must be allowed to grow in the field alongside the wheat until the harvest, but when the harvest comes they will certainly not be gathered into the garner, but only rooted up as worthless and fit for burning. Belonging to the Catholic Church, believing all it believes, using all its sacraments, gives to no one the guarantee of salvation. On the other hand, there are many not only outside the visible Church, however widely defined, but outside Christianity altogether, in fact outside any religious belief, who, because of their desire for truth, their acts of interior contrition, their attempts to serve their fellows, do belong to the soul of the Church, are numbered among the elect, and, if in this life they never attain to the full light of revelation, yet, because of their interior readiness to receive it, on beholding it at last will accept it, and so attain to the light of glory. Indeed, it can be held that full conscious membership in the organized body of the Catholic Church exposes anyone who is not

THE CHURCH AND HUMANITY

faithful to greater risk and condemnation than not to be in it at all, if, nevertheless, one is faithful to all that one sees and believes. This admission does not for a moment relieve anyone from his obvious duty, who possesses the light to recognize the truths of Christianity and the claims of the Catholic Church. It is not difficult to see that the Mystical Church can only be discerned because of the visible Church, and it is the purpose of the organized Church to bring individuals into conscious contact with the saving soul of the Church. Hence it is not remarkable that the Catholic, while standing rigidly for the necessity of the Church, will often have far wider hopes for the rest of humanity than those who belong to the smaller sects. But the better understanding of this doctrine, which would come about if only it was published more widely and proclaimed more emphatically, would certainly have the effect of drawing many more to the Church and of bringing about the reconciliation of all Christians in the Catholic Church. It is the false idea of what is meant by the Church's exclusiveness that keeps so many people out; they feel quite unable to claim a privileged position for themselves if it also compels them to believe that others are lost because they cannot honestly accept the conditions under which these privileges are supposed to be alone available.

A better understanding of the claims of the Catholic Church and the demands of faith could be brought about if something could be done to make clearer the conditions of belief. If the Protestant attempts at the solution of this problem are to be described as unsuccessful, much has yet to be done on the Catholic side to make clearer what is meant by believing what the Church believes, and because the Church believes it; not only to relieve that ground

THE CHURCH AND HUMANITY

of acceptance from any suspicion of intellectual evasion or slothfulness, but also in order to prevent the beliefs thus accepted from being accepted unintelligently, and therefore remaining ineffectual. Something could be done to ease the condition of those whose loyalty to Christ and desire to be reckoned as His are beyond any doubt, and whose difficulty about certain of the Church's beliefs is not really intellectual, but arises from a misunderstanding of the kind of belief that the Church demands. This is a task which can only be undertaken by the Roman Catholic authorities: first of all, because the situation is so often misrepresented by Roman controversialists. Sometimes it might almost be gathered from their attitude towards believers outside that they have no right to believe any Christian doctrine unless they believe it on the sole and simple ground that the Church teaches it; that is, that no one save themselves has any right to a single article of the Christian faith. For if anyone comes to a belief from study of the Scriptures, consideration of the rational argument, and prayer for guidance, and yet is doubtful about other things that the Roman Catholic Church demands, there is a disposition to condemn such an attitude as religiously worthless. Secondly, it is only where there is such an instrument of authoritative utterance as the Roman Church possesses that any such statement can carry sufficient weight and influence. For even to Protestants, who may reject as untrue what Rome teaches, that authoritative utterance does tell what Rome does actually teach; whereas Protestant Churches confessedly possess no instrument of equal authority even for themselves. In particular, if some Roman scholars would only set themselves to clear up the present considerable ambiguity about faith they would do an immense service to their own communion, hasten reunion, and clear away a great stumbling-block from the path of those who are seeking the truth. What needs to be shown is what part is played in the faith that saves, first by the exercise of reason, open to every person guided by common sense, which should lead to belief in the existence of God, the historicity of Christ, His claim to divinity, and His promise to build His Church upon the rock; secondly, what is the nature, place and effect of that faith which can only be the gift of God, and what is necessary to receive it; finally, what is the nature of the belief which makes it possible to believe what the Church believes, and how far that is prior to, or is a result of divine faith, or how far it reposes upon or is different from common-sense rational acceptance of facts. The world is not being given a fair chance to believe, because of the confusion which exists on this issue, which much current controversy between Catholics and Protestants only intensifies.

A still greater hindrance to reunion would be removed if the authorities of the Roman Catholic Church would clearly, utterly and dogmatically disavow any further recourse to persecution. It is here their claim to be the one lineal descendant of the historic Church places them under a heavier liability, while their power of promulgating an irreformable decree makes it possible for them to make such a final statement and give such a future guarantee as certainly no one else possesses, which the world must have if a not unfounded fear is to be allayed. It may be that Protestants too often forget that they once equally accepted the idea that persecution was allowable in the interests of religion, but then Protestantism is not tied, as is the Roman Church,

THE CHURCH AND HUMANITY

to the past. And it is therefore not merely ignorance of history or an accident of memory that the persecution of Protestants by Romans is made a charge against Rome, while the persecution of Romans by Protestants is ignored. It would be quite possible to maintain that in the past God has allowed bigamy and slavery which Christianity, nevertheless, does not permit; that He has used war, which an awakened Christianity is now beginning to believe cannot any longer be sanctioned for Christians by the law of charity; that He has used persecution to protect truth and repress error, but in all these cases only because of the hardness of men's hearts and their inability at that time to rise to a higher ideal. But some assurance needs to be given, beyond any now existing, that persecution is from henceforth abandoned, because man has reached a stage of higher responsibility and of personal development wherein the wrong of persecution would be not so much in its employment of pain and threat, as in the endangering of the perfectly free and unbiased choice of religion, which is necessary if faith is to be real and effective. Persecution is a wrong done, not to the body of man, but to his soul.

By some such action as this the Church could make clear the reality of its humanitarian concern, show itself true to its own charter, and immensely hasten the spread of faith and the progress of humanity. It is growing clearer that mere humanitarianism, despite its ideals, its promises and the actual gains to its credit, is no true friend of humanity. The value of humanity is not in itself, but in its end, namely, in the attainment of a perfect life of union together in God. If the Divine creation of man and the realization of its purpose in eternal life are denied, man is reduced at once to the level of the

THE CHURCH AND HUMANITY

animal, and the very word humanitarian becomes a meaningless and unscientific term, and would only designate a concern for animals, which is precisely what humanitarianism so often comes to mean. The standard of humanity is not in empirical humanity as it now exists, but in Christ, God become man. The highest valuation that can be placed upon man is not due to anything in himself, but to the value put upon him by Christ when He died for every man. Nowhere else can there be found a real basis for democracy, from which the world hopes so much, save in the eternal value of every soul, and the necessity for seeing that it has power to render unconfused obedience to its supreme Head and King, Jesus Christ, unhindered by society, government or State. Nowhere, save in the Christian redemption, can we find any real principle that will guarantee the preservation of the undeveloped tribes of the earth, which a selfish and short-sighted commercial civilization would not only exploit, but soon destroy, as it has already done. The protection of native races reposes solely on the belief that they have their right and their value in humanity, because they can be baptized into the Triune Name and be illuminated by the Spirit, even as others before them, who owe all their advance to that very Gospel they are now beginning to neglect. A much humaner treatment of animals is needed in Christendom, but this must not be founded on the theory that they are as important as man, or that all life is one, but that man has been given an undoubted lordship over them, for which, however, he will have to give a strict account. The Christian religion, and more particularly the Catholic emphasis, holds that man's earthly life is a preparation for eternity, and the manner of his earthly life determines the condition of his eternal destiny: and faith is not, as some early Protestant doctrines held, a substitute for a worthy life on earth, or a passport into heaven: faith produces the worthy life and finally makes a man fit for heavenly existence. Thus Christianity is seen to be the true humanitarianism, because it has stamped humanity with the valuation given to it by the Incarnation and the Cross of Christ. The Church is thus the guardian of humanity's freedom, progress and hope. The Catholic Church is the only supra-national and supra-human entity in which all nations and all men can hope to find a meeting-place and a ground of higher unity. The Roman Catholic Church, because of its historic position, its dogmatic attitude, its authoritative basis and its world-wide diffusion, is the core of Christianity, and holds the key to a door which it can either open or shut. Its historic position gives it not only culture, riches and prestige; it places upon it the responsibility for purging the past; its dogmatic attitude can provide guarantees that an emancipating word can never be rescinded; its authoritative basis promises more hope of obedience; and its world-wide diffusion gives to its decrees a power that cannot be disputed by nationalistic States.

The recognition given, in this present discussion and those which have preceded it, to the place and importance of the Roman Church, may be unwelcome to the more contented and hostile type of Protestant, but it has only been accorded because it seems true to the actual facts of the situation. If, however, it is admitted that Rome holds the key, it does not follow that the key is being rightly used. It does indeed look as if she is using the key to guard the central treasure of Christianity, and for that all Christians should be thankful; for in the present confusion and temptation some-

THE CHURCH AND HUMANITY

one must stand firm for the one faith and the one Church. But it does not look as if the key was being used to open the doors of the Church as wide as possible to needy and seeking humanity. Ever since the Protestant revolt, and no doubt because of the tendency of Protestantism to fall away more and more from the faith, a spirit of panic seems to have swayed the Roman Church, and every doorway is locked and barred, not only in fear of any further defection, but as if to prevent any re-entrance of the principles which produced Protestantism. But surely the defection of Protestantism can be traced in the first instance to alarm at a worldly corruption, a tolerance of immorality and a growth of superstition which seemed likely to overwhelm the Christian faith. And surely the most rigid and complacent Roman apologist must be driven to admit that while the divisions of Protestantism seem only to mark a way out into the ultimate wilderness of unbelief, they also mark a way back; for do not the Protestant Churches provide by far the greater majority of converts to Rome ? In the present state of advancing unbelief, the indifference of the masses in all civilized countries, the feeble condition of modern faith, could even the most bigoted Roman controversialist welcome the disappearance of all or any of the Protestant Churches ? Does not this point a moral to both sides to seek a reconciliation for the sake of humanity ?

It is no narrow ecclesiastical interest or partisan concern that has prompted our attempt to point out where the foundations of faith are to be found, nor even a concern for the mere triumph of Christianity, but rather a tremendous concern for the present salvation and future hope of humanity. It seems to us that at present, owing largely to Protestant and Catholic controversy, humanity is

THE CHURCH AND HUMANITY

not having even a chance of seeing Christianity, or of knowing what the faith is. The call must be to Rome in the first instance, because until she does something, the hindrance remains. She is doing much at present by defending the rational basis of natural theology, and this is of special value in the prevalence of irrational scepticism; she is doing much also to open out to all seekers of an authenticating religious experience the true pathway of prayer and the way of holiness. It is, however, in the realm that lies between, and especially in the presentation of a generous ecclesiasticism, that much now needs to be done. But for this there will be needed not only apologetics and explanation on the subject of the Church; there will be needed ecclesiastical action to confirm it, and so present to the unshepherded multitude a Church informed through all its organizations by an identifiable Christian spirit, seeking not its own, but the salvation of souls, offering that to men by presenting to them Christ, unclouded by superstition, unaccompanied by irrelevant conditions, unconfused by threats or bribes; a Church which is obviously able to be the home of all humanity, the inspirer of all true progress, emancipation and release, the defender of the poor, the restrainer of the proud, the reconciler of the hostile and the estranged, the eternal rock on which can be built the city of God and the kingdom of Christ.

For Product Safety Concerns and Information please contact our EU representative GPSR@taylorandfrancis.com
Taylor & Francis Verlag GmbH, Kaufingerstraße 24, 80331 München, Germany

www.ingramcontent.com/pod-product-compliance
Lightning Source LLC
Chambersburg PA
CBHW050635300426
44112CB00012B/1813